What Others Have Said

I have been completely changed by these stories in A Journey with Christ. God has shown me that children belong to Him. The Bible says that the kingdom of God belongs to such as these (little children). The beauty of this book is that it simply shows us that we need to become like little children so that we can see heaven. If you must be encouraged to have faith in God, this book will encourage you as it has encouraged me.

Janet Chola-Mbugua, Mnjala's mother

I am sure at some point in most people's lives, whether religious or not, you have wondered whether heaven exists and if there really is a God. After hearing the incredible stories of Mungai and his cousin Mnjala's frequent trips to heaven—the amazing things they have seen, relatives they have met in heaven, lessons that Jesus taught them, and predictions that have come true—we no longer have to doubt the existence of heaven and God. It is real, and by their descriptions, it's even more amazing than you can imagine!

Hazel Anderson

When I initially heard these stories, I thought them unbelievable. How could Jesus appear to such young babes, but then again, why not? The children give details of things that are out of this world, things they could not have learned in Sunday school or formal school. My family and I totally believe these stories, and our relationship with God has gone to a higher level. I am personally just foolish for God. When I read the word of God, I just believe it, claim it, and profess it. I feel so excited and have so much warmth in my heart that this book has finally come to fruition. I pray it will help you believe in the existence of God but, above all, bring you to the realization that you can do nothing apart from Him. May it propel you to greater heights in a wonderful, loving relationship with the Creator of this universe.

Angella N. Githere wa Langat

Thanks to my nephew Mungai's visitations and very detailed descriptions, my perception of God, who was for a very long time an abstract being who lived way up in heaven, has now changed. I have come to know that God is real. He is my very own Heavenly Father. He cares for and loves me. I am made in His image, and I believe that heaven and hell do truly exist. This, for me, is no longer a farfetched myth but a reality. Heaven is a beautiful place where love, joy, peace, and harmony prevail, while hell is a scary place where there is pain, darkness, evil, and hatred. The decision regarding where I spend eternity depends on me. This reality has made me want to seek an intimate love relationship with God while I am on earth so I can meet Him in heaven one day and live happily ever after. On the other hand, the truth about hell has made my heart sensitive to those who do not know God. I am pained that, if I do not share information about God and His salvation with them, they are doomed for eternity. I can no longer be complacent but must actively share the good news of salvation with them. Moreover, the love of God for my family awes me. My mother, who loved God dearly, passed away on January 4, 2011. That night, the Lord showed my mother worshiping God in the throne room to my nephew. Though I knew my mother had gone to be with the Lord, this confirmed that she was truly with her maker. This experience really touched the rest of the family and me to know that God in His own mercy would go out of His way to confirm where our mother is. I was so comforted, and from that point onward, I felt a peace that I cannot describe even to this day. I really thank God for so graciously choosing a member of my family to make these fundamental truths a reality to me.

Annie Kinuthia

Narrated in this book are the details of the several visits to heaven and hell that two young boys continue to make. The stories make spiritual experiences so accessible and encourage those of us who desire these experiences to want them even more. Each chapter is a progression from the other, culminating in the ultimate revelation of Christ to us all. This book will teach you about the reserves that God has for all our needs up in heaven and how powerful He is. You will also learn that heaven and hell are real because the two boys have seen them and confirm the existence of both. May the simplicity of the redemption story and the Father's love for all humankind come alive as you read.

Linda Maruti

Lydia came to me one early morning at work and told me that something strange happened to her son. Then she explained how he had seen two angels at their gate at home. Being a mother myself, I felt her concern, and we started praying and asking God to reveal what it was all about. Little did we know that it was the beginning of an extraordinary journey. This experience has changed my prayer life and my perspective of God. It has given me a drive to ensure that nobody misses heaven. I talk about God everywhere I go and share this experience whenever I get a chance to. I have shared it with family and friends. My highlights have been the two times I shared at funeral services, and suddenly there was a change in the way of mourning as hope was registered in every heart. Being human, I have asked myself how I would react if Jesus suddenly appeared where I was. I had a mental picture of how I would carry myself until the day He appeared while we were driving. I suddenly went numb, and I could not even think. However, the truth is that Jesus is right there with us every time we call on Him. Read on, and be blessed. Most importantly, ensure that nobody around you misses heaven!

Esther Kathuri

For many years, I have desired to understand the message of heaven and hell and to at least learn about the God of the Bible. I believe in the God of the Bible, and I also believe that heaven and hell are real places. Though I believed this, I didn't really comprehend that these places exist and they are real until I heard the story of Mungai and Mnjala. For the past two years, I have greatly enjoyed and benefited from the fascinating stories and messages laced with life principles and truth. The messages that are still very clear to me are firstly the torment, pain, and gnashing of teeth in hell, which stirred up a passion for souls within me. It was reaffirmed to me that, while I'm in this world, I'm not of this world and I belong to a higher kingdom, the heavenly kingdom of which I am an ambassador to this world. Thus by developing my spirit and renewing my mind by the word of God, I can release His life to others and be a powerful witness for the kingdom of God. The second story is the one that Mnjala gave. Jesus told him to wake up and prepare himself to go for Sunday school, telling him that life is not about eating and drinking, thus he should go and hear God's Word. This confirmed John 1:14 ("The Word became flesh and made His dwelling among us. We have seen His glory, the glory of the One and Only who came from the Father full of grace and truth"). When I read, study, meditate on, or confess the word of God, I am fellowshipping with Jesus. I am actually taking Him as nourishment, and I find that only He alone can satisfy my soul. God's Word is my spiritual food, and I need it regularly, just as I need natural food. The last thing I have learned from these two boys' stories and messages is their simple childlike faith in God, which is just amazing. It has really inspired me to believe God, no matter what. Every day is a walk of faith at some level. Everyone believes in something. God has dealt to each one a measure of faith (Rom. 12:3). We choose what we will believe in. Faith is something we cannot live without. Our faith determines what happens to us after we leave this world. If we have faith in Jesus, you know that your eternal future is secure. We all need to do our best, work hard and live wisely, but we must also have faith in God, trusting Him to see us through difficulties, show us how to live, provide for us, and guide us in the affairs of our daily lives. We cannot please God without faith (Heb. 11:6). In simple terms, these children have challenged me to reevaluate my level of trust in God by seeing them trust God and take Him at His Word without reasoning with Him. Thank you, Mungai and Mnjala, for these messages that have helped shape my life. My prayer is that this book will help you to see life with a fresh, new perspective. You see that God loves every person and He wants to do everyone good. The Bible pretty well sums it up. "For God so loved the world that He gave His one and only Son." The Bible also says that God is love (1 John 4:8). Because of this great love, each willing person can receive salvation, healing, deliverance, peace, blessings, and every other good thing God promises us in His Word. Remember, God has given us the power of choice. We must choose one way or the other, and whatever pathway we choose will lead to a specific destination (Deut. 11:26–28). Thank you, Mama Mungai. It was an honor to share.

Rikanda Njoki, Eagle's Faith Christian Centre

God is using the lips of babes to speak to the church. God, heaven, and hell are real, and we ought to focus on the gospel of repentance and not just on the gospel of prosperity. We need to know that there is a better life in heaven after death if you believe in Jesus. The Bible spells out everything that the Lord has shown Mungai and Mnjala. The Bible is the true word of God.

Carol Njeru, Eagle's Faith Christian Centre

I am the head usher at Eagle's Faith Christian Centre. When I first met Lydia, I thought she was reserved. She requested me to allow her to sit at the back of the church, and because I knew she was a first-time visitor, I heeded her request. She continued to attend church together with her son, and one day, Pastor George called her forward and prophesied over her life. After some time, Pastor George requested Lydia and Mungai to testify, and that was the first time I heard of the visitations from Jesus Christ. I listened in amazement. I could hardly wait to ask her what else had happened. We began talking, and I must confess the testimony of Mungai has changed my perception of God the Father, Jesus Christ, and the Holy Spirit. One of the stories that changed my life was when Lydia shared about how Mungai and his cousin Mnjala visited heaven, and as they were playing, they heard a loud voice calling them. They instantly knew that it was God the Father calling them. When they entered the throne room, God ushered them to golden seats set before Him, and He asked them to sit down. God the Father then squeezed honey from His hands and gave it to the two boys. He asked them to eat. And as Lydia told me, the boys said it was the yummiest honey they had ever tasted. This story had such a profound impact on me because, at the time, I had been going through a difficult period and asking God many questions. As I listened to Lydia, I felt hope rise within me. God used her words to remind me that He was concerned about everything that I was going through. And just as He had given the two boys the sweetest honey to eat, He would also give me the sweetest honey that I needed then. As I listen to Lydia testify more and more about the encounters that the boys have had, my faith has been strengthened, my hope has been renewed, and I can truly say, "I can hardly wait to get to heaven!"

Maureen Kabure, Eagle's Faith Christian Centre

In 2009, when my husband and I came to Kenya to visit my family, we were at my sister Lydia's house in Westlands, Nairobi. One evening, we had all gone to bed, but I was very restless, so I decided to go to my sister's room because I knew she was not yet asleep. As I told her about me being restless and not being able to sleep, she suggested that we pray. We talked about my nephews' stories about heaven and God. I believed in Jesus. My sister then told me to ask God for whatever I wanted. So I said, "All I really want is a good job with nice colleagues and a nice boss." We prayed, and I just realized I was crying. I just opened my heart to God. After that, we went to bed, and I slept peacefully. My husband and I spent the rest of the holiday in Kenya until January 4, 2010. When we returned to Germany on or about January 15, I read this job advert on the Internet, and I immediately applied for the position. While I was writing, I kept praying, "God, give me this job." Three days later, the human resources department called my home, but I was not home. The person on the other end talked to my husband and said he would call back later. He called three times and missed me. Please note, most companies here in Europe do conduct a telephone interview before inviting someone to the real personal interview. So I told my husband that, if he were to call again, he should just arrange with him where I should meet him. A few days later, I was on my way to the interview. I have never been so calm, and the interview went so well. We talked and laughed, and it all took over two hours. On January 29, I was just at the parking lot, ready to open the car to drive back home from work, when my mobile phone rang. Note, I always have my cell phone off, but on this particular day, I had somehow forgotten to put it off at work. "Welcome on board" was the first sentence I heard after picking up my phone. I just screamed and said a big "Thank you!" to God. This was the best day ever because I was so very sure that there is a God who hears and answers. I have a nice boss, wonderful colleagues, and a very good job.

Esther Chola-Thommes

The Chola family has been close to our family. We attended church together with Mrs. Chola, Lydia's mother, at Gospel Tabernacle Christian Centre in the 1990s. Mrs. Chola was a close friend and prayer partner to my mother. I remember how charismatic she was and how she loved God with all her heart. It comes as no surprise that her children, Grace, Lydia, Pastor Chola, and others, have grown up to be godly men and women serving the Lord Jesus Christ. Her grandson Mungai has stepped into a whole new level with supernatural revelations from the Lord Jesus Christ Himself. Similar revelations, which corroborate Mungai's experiences, have been given to different people worldwide. In Matthew 11:25, Jesus says, "I praise to you, Father, Lord of heaven and earth, because you have hidden these things from the wise and learned, and revealed them to little children." This has literally happened in the life of Mungai.

Alex Kathuri Kiara

We have followed the young boys' testimonies for well over a year, and even when the boys are apart, their testimonies remain the same. We thank God for His great work in the lives of Mungai and Mnjala, who happen to be our nephews. The Bible says, "A child shall lead them" (Isa. 11:6). We pray you will be changed by these stories and change others around you. God bless!

Mr. and Mrs. Kamau

This is an amazing story! It is comforting to know that, although it was in the Bible times that Jesus asked the little children to come to Him, He is still doing it today. This story makes the supernatural so real. It has firmed my desire to surrender my life more to God so that, when eternity comes, I shall be in His presence, no longer by faith, but by sight. Thank you, Lydia, for taking the step to write this book.

W.W, Counseling Psychologist, Nairobi, Kenya

Listening to the children's experience reminds one that the spiritual world is real and we are not the only ones in control. This is a revelation that everything that happens in the physical begins in the spiritual. It's amazing, exciting, and so reassuring as a constant reminder of God's presence, goodness, faithfulness, and, ultimately, His invincible might. It brings God and heaven out of the fairy tales and into our practical day-to-day life. We thank God that He has revealed Himself yet again through little children.

Rebah Sijenyi

I heard the stories, I believed them, and I still believe. It is impossible for little children to make up such stories. But the greatest lesson for me is that all these stories tally with the Bible, the infallible word of God. Surely the Christian faith has never come so close home!

Zenah Nyathama

It's an amazing revelation (once again) that God loves me so much that it's enough to send a message of hope and in such a humble way.

Mary Njagi

I head the Sunday school Ministry at Eagles Faith Christian Center. Mungai and Mnjala have shared about their experiences of heaven and angels in the Sunday school class. I have learnt a lot from these children. What amazes me is the fact that they just say it as it is. They do not try to convince anyone, there is such innocence in what they say. Everything they have shared is in line with God's word because the Lord wants to use little children to teach us who He is. I believe and know that what the children have seen is true.

I noticed that every time I asked the Sunday school children to color pictures of Jesus, the other children would paint Him brown while Mungai and Mnjala would paint Jesus in yellow. His face, hands and feet would be colored yellow too. When I asked them why they paint Jesus in yellow, they told me that it is because it is the closest color they can think of that looks like Jesus. "Jesus shines." They always tell me.

Dorothy Mulinge, Eagle's Faith Christian Center

A revelation of heaven and hell... the reality of their existence... Who would have thought that this truth would have been made clear and real to a little boy somewhere in the middle of Nairobi? Who would have thought that this same little boy, Mungai would have dreams and in spirit, meet with His majesty, the Lord and Savior, Jesus Christ? And once more, who would have thought that this same little boy would share the same revelations with his first cousin, another little boy, Mnjala?

The Bible says in Joe 2:28, '...your young men will see visions'. The Lord God is pouring His Spirit on His people. The Lord God is convicting hearts and speaking to men, women and children to choose eternal life and escape damnation. From the mouths of babes, we are being reminded of the reality of heaven and hell.

We have all sinned and fall short of the glory of God (Romans 3:23). Let's choose eternal life in heaven! Thank God for His unconditional love!

Liza Kamwithi-Mulamula

A Journey with Christ

A Journey with Christ

Lydia Chola-Waiyaki

WESTBOW
PRESS
A DIVISION OF THOMAS NELSON

ISBN: 978-1-4497-5861-5 (sc)
ISBN: 978-1-4497-5862-2 (hc)
ISBN: 978-1-4497-5860-8 (e)

WestBow Press books may be ordered through booksellers or by contacting:

WestBow Press
A Division of Thomas Nelson
1663 Liberty Drive
Bloomington, IN 47403
www.westbowpress.com
1-(866) 928-1240

Scripture taken from the HOLY BIBLE, NEW INTERNATIONAL
VERSION. Copyright 1973, 1978, 1984 by International Bible
Society. Used by permission of Zondervan. All rights reserved.

Library of Congress Control Number: 2012912164

Printed in the United States of America

WestBow Press rev. date: 7/25/2012

A Journey with Christ

*A true story of how Our Lord Jesus Christ
showed two young boys heaven and hell.*

Lydia Chola-Waiyaki

To Our Lord Jesus Christ, the King of kings and Lord of lords, without whom I would be lost and hopeless. I am forever grateful to Him for what He did on the cross for all of us and for me. May this book bring honor and glory to His mighty and glorious name. Amen.

Contents

Foreword

I have had a lot of time to think about the foreword Lydia asked me to write for her book. What a privilege for me to contribute to this awesome project. As I pen my words, I cannot seem to get my mind off the fact that, for days now, the media houses around the world have been reporting on the tragic death of the music legend, Whitney Houston, on February 11, 2012. The details surrounding her demise have been sketchy, but they all report that she died in a hotel bathroom. They say she began her singing career in church. As tributes flow from all over the world in honor of the troubled star, I have been thinking, "Where is Whitney? Did she know the Lord Jesus?"

The encounters the two young boys continue to have and their visits to heaven from their beds have had a profound impact on my life and our church. I am both excited and in awe of the magnitude of the mission the Lord Jesus has placed upon our ministry. What a joy to know that the testimonies that began in our small congregation will now be read in many nations of the world.

According to Scripture, a man is spirit, soul, and body. 1 Thessalonians 5:23 says, "May God Himself the God of peace, sanctify you through and through May your whole spirit, soul and body be kept blameless at the coming of our Lord Jesus Christ." The spirit of man is the real man created in the image and likeness of God. The soul of man includes his reasoning faculties. But the real man is the spirit man that was created to fellowship with God in God's realm, which is the realm of the Spirit. It is also referred to as the eternal realm or faith realm. Your mind and body are merely instruments of the real you. Your senses can only perceive a physical or material realm but cannot connect to the eternal, spiritual world.

Ephesians 6 talks about the spiritual warfare all around us, from which our sense organs receive no sensation. Our physical senses are completely unaware of the presence of the Holy Spirit or the mighty angels that watch over you and me. At death, the real man and his soul leave the body. When this happens, the body has no more reason for existing, and disintegration sets in immediately.

There was a time you were not, but there will never be a time that you shall not be. Five hundred years from now, you shall be alive somewhere. The way you live your life on earth determines where you will spend eternity!

Teach us to number our days aright, that we may gain a heart of wisdom.

Psalm 90:12

Pastor George Mathu, Eagles Faith Christian Centre
Nairobi, Kenya

Preface

Dear reader, what you are about to read is not a regular story. It is an incredibly amazing true story that has come from the mouths of young children, my nephew, Mnjala Mbugua, who was seven years old at the time of the writing of this book, and my son, Mungai Waiyaki, who was eight. The two boys are cousins. They were born exactly a year apart on October 29 in Nairobi, Kenya.

This story is, however, not about the two boys. It is about God Almighty, the Creator of heaven and earth and everything in it. The story will prove to you that God is real and His Son, Jesus Christ, is real. It will clear any doubt in your mind that God made you. He loves you and wants to have a loving relationship with you through His Son, Jesus. You will come to the knowledge and understanding of a special place called heaven, a place that this mighty God has prepared for those who love and fear Him and are living in accordance to His Word.

Amazingly, God has used little children to reveal Himself to us. These two children do not live in the same home, but Our Lord Jesus in his power and might picks them from their beds at the same time during the night and takes them to heaven. They have also been taken to hell several times. On each trip to either heaven or hell, they are taught incredible truths that are in the word of God, the Bible.

I am Mungai's mother. This book began as a diary that I was keeping for him when it became increasingly obvious to me that God was beginning something extraordinary in his life. It was imperative to record the unusual events, and I did this in chronological order as they unfolded. What was interesting was that, each time my son would narrate an event about heaven or hell, he would talk about his cousin Mnjala. He would tell me that they had been together, and I would excitedly call my sister, Janet Mbugua, Mnjala's mother, who would recount to me the exact stories from her son. Little Mnjala would then relate to me the same incidents that Mungai had told me. How incredible!

I have on several occasions wondered why us, my son, my nephew, or our family, but I have realized that God is sovereign and He decides who and how His Word is to be spread. I also realized that one of the prophecies in the Old Testament, Joel 2:28, is being fulfilled. "And afterwards, I will pour out my Spirit on all people. Your sons and daughters will prophesy, your old men will dream dreams, your young men will see visions." Indeed, this is exactly what is happening to young Mungai and Mnjala.

I have been sharing these wonderful stories because Jesus has changed my life through the children's visions. Many who have heard some of the stories you are about to read have also claimed a change in their lives. I pray, you too, will open your heart and, like a little child, let God speak to you. Your life will never be the same again!

Acknowledgments

I thank God for giving me the courage and strength to write this book. It was a most challenging experience, but God watched over everything in order to get His work accomplished. I want to thank my son, Mungai, for being patient while I put the book together. I thank both Mungai and Mnjala for providing the backbone stories for this book. It has been a joy, honor, and blessing to watch God use them in this way.

I thank my husband, Waiyaki Mungai, for ensuring that I got all the tools and finances I needed for writing. I thank him also for taking the lead in designing the cover of the book. I want to acknowledge my dad and my mum, Duncan and Kezia Mnjala Chola, who raised me up in the fear of God. Thank you especially, dear Mum, for your prayers. You have prayed for me all the days of my life. Mum, the vision you saw concerning me is coming to pass.

I give my sincere gratitude to my parents-in-law, Parmenus and Joyce Mungai. They were so excited when they heard I was writing a book, and they gave me all their support, encouragement, and prayers.

I thank God for you my sister, Janet Mbugua. God used you to confirm to me that I should write this book. God bless you for encouraging me to pursue God's calling and for your prayers and support.

I have much appreciation for my dear friend and colleague, Esther Kathuri. You have been a source of encouragement and support for me. Thank you especially for your prayers and for allowing God to use your special gifts to uphold me.

I want to thank my good friend, Zenah Angela Nyathama, for being there for me throughout the writing of this book. You encouraged me and prayed for me, but most of all, thank you for editing this book. Zenah, I cannot express how grateful I am for all the hours you put into it. May our God in heaven richly reward you. Special thanks to Winnie Waiyaki for providing some editorial assistance.

I gratefully recognize and credit those at WestBow Press [A division of Thomas Nelson] at Bloomington Indiana who have been instrumental in making this book from God available to the readers.

Finally, I would like to thank Pastor George Mathu, our very dear pastor. Thank you for cheering me on while I wrote and for giving me direction and sound advice. You caught the vision of the book, and you ran with it! Thank you for accepting my request and writing the foreword. You believed in me, and you have helped Mungai and Mnjala to not only grow in the Lord but to also be confident in whom they are in God. You are an integral part of their lives. We thank God for you! The prophecy you gave a few weeks after my mother had a dream about me tallied with the dream that was about God raising me up higher. I would never have imagined that God would bring such a special blessing to my life. I will forever be grateful to Our Lord and King, Jesus Christ.

Introduction

On the morning of October 14, 2010, my sister told me about the vision she had the previous night. That morning, as I was leaving the house, I read Psalm 32:8. "I will instruct you and teach you in the way you should go; I will counsel you and watch over you." I pondered over those words as I reversed out of my parking space at my house. Well, I did not know that God was literally going to instruct me on what I should do on that very day.

I had made it a habit to pray for my son each morning as I drove him to school. You will read why this had become a normal part of our routine. When we got to our destination, I bid him good-bye and proceeded to my workplace. My cell phone alerted me that I had received a text message.

I thought, *Who is sending me a text message so early in the morning?*

As soon as I pulled into the parking area at my workplace, I got out my phone to read the message. My sister Janet told me that she had a vision concerning me during the night. She said that Jesus had shown her some events that would take place in my life. She saw everything very clearly, but the last part of her message made my heart beat faster.

"Then you wrote a book—*A Journey with Christ*—it was explaining the stories of our children, but all was for the glory of Jesus."

I immediately called her, and we had a very interesting conversation. She told me that God wanted me to write and she had already seen a completed copy, a beautiful book shining like gold with its title glaring at her. Even more inspiring was the fact that she gave me the title of the book. I was not sure of what title to give it when I began, but I had initially written "An Incredible Journey with Jesus" on every other page because I felt we were on a journey with God and the title needed to depict this. How loudly God had spoken to me that very day. I had to obey.

Yet another confirmation came my way as I was winding up the writing of this book. During the festive season of December 2011, Mungai, Mnjala, and I were seated in a restaurant having dinner. In the course of dinner, Mnjala surprised me by casually informing me that he had seen my book in heaven. I was so amazed. He said that Our Lord, Jesus, had taken him to the library in heaven and shown him the finished book, which was lying on a shelf in between two Bibles. Jesus picked the book from the shelf and showed Mnjala the front and back cover of the book.

Mnjala was so surprised that he asked Jesus, "The book is ready?"

Jesus replied, "Yes, the book is complete in heaven!"

When I heard this, I cried with joy. In my heart, I thanked God that I had obeyed Him.

As soon as we got home, I showed Mnjala the cover sample.

He casually assured me, "Yes, that is what I saw in heaven. There was a picture of a bed on the front cover of the book and your picture on the back."

Three days later, on December 14, 2011, Mnjala was taken up to heaven again. This time, he was in the throne room of God.

God the Father said to him from His throne, "I am very happy with the book, and it will change many peoples' lives."

Gladness filled my heart when I heard this good news from my little nephew. God had confirmed yet again that it was His will that this book be written.

The children have continued to have visitations during and after the writing of this book, some of which have not been captured here.

So here is the true account of the two boys who Our Lord Jesus Christ has visited many times and repeatedly shown them heaven and hell. This same Jesus wants you to believe in Him. God bless you!

At that time Jesus said, "I praise you, Father, Lord of heaven and earth, because you have hidden these things from the wise and learned, and revealed them to little children. Yes, Father, for this was your good pleasure."
Matthew 11:25–26

Chapter 1

Angels at the Gate

I will never forget August 19, 2009. I woke up to a day of sweet surprises from highly unexpected quarters. I had never expected anything supernatural to take place in our home, but it did. This was the beginning of an incredible journey with Our Lord Jesus, whose magnitude I was not even aware of.

I was seated on my bed reading my Bible when Mungai, my son, and Mnjala, my nephew, rushed into my room holding plastic toy swords in their hands.

My son was shouting, "Mum, two angels were at the gate at night!"

I thought, *What is he talking about?*

Then my son noticed I was not paying attention to him and held my face. "I know the names of the two angels. They are called Angel Gabriel and Angel Michael."

His words caught my attention because these two angels have been mentioned several times in the Bible. In the book of Daniel, it is recorded that Daniel prayed to God, but the answer was delayed because the princes of darkness wanted to stop the

1

message God was sending to him. Gabriel came against these great forces for twenty-one days and was delayed because the demons had gathered to hinder him. The demons were trying to stop the end-time message from reaching Daniel. Finally, the Holy Spirit sent Michael, the great warring angel in command of all warring angels. Because of Michael's tremendous spiritual might, he was able to push back the opposing forces of darkness. "But the prince of the Persian kingdom resisted me twenty-one days. Then Michael, one of the chief princes, came to help me, because I was detained there with the king of Persia" (Dan. 10:13).

In the New Testament, Luke 1:26–38 records the famous story about the birth of Jesus. Angel Gabriel is the mighty angel who God sent to the Virgin Mary to deliver the good news about the birth of Jesus Christ.

"How did you know the names of the angels?" I asked Mungai.

"When I saw them, I knew in my heart who they were."

The two boys said Angel Michael was at the right side of the gate holding his sword facing upwards, while Angel Gabriel was on the left side of the gate with his sword pointing downwards. The boys stood on either side of the window demonstrating how these angels were positioned at the gate with fiery swords in their hands. The children showed me the top part of their toy swords and told me that the angels' swords had fire on that part of their swords.

My son said excitedly, "Mum, their eyes ... the eyes of the angels were shining so much. They were at the gate, but they could still see us. Mum, we were still in our bed. I could also see the guard at the gate, but I don't think he could see the angels. The angels were so big that they were much taller than the gate."

"Were you scared?" I asked.

"No, Mum, I was not scared. I was so happy. I thought God was going to take me to heaven!"

His response completely stunned me, but I nevertheless asked, "What were the angels wearing?"

They quickly answered in unison, "Shining white!"

The boys described the angels' attire. They said they had white clothes that looked like dresses but were not. Big belts around their waists were made out of gold, and fiery swords were in their hands. This description of the angels coming from the children is truly amazing because it is found in the Bible in the book of Daniel. "I looked up and there before me was a man dressed in linen, with a belt of the finest gold around his waist. His body was like chrysolite, his face like lightning, his eyes like flaming torches, his arms and legs like the gleam of burnished bronze, and his voice like the sound of a multitude" (Dan. 10:5-6).

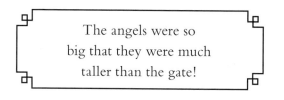

The angels were so big that they were much taller than the gate!

Wow, I thought, *what a mighty God we serve!*

I sat on my bed for a long time, wondering, pondering, and feeling amazed. I couldn't keep this news to myself, so I telephoned my mother and then my sister, Janet, Mnjala's mum. She did not seem at all surprised, as she was accustomed to her son telling her a lot about God, angels, and heaven. Mnjala had several encounters with the supernatural from the time he could talk, as I will explain later in this book. My mother, on the other hand, was so excited. She kept praising God as I went on and on about the angels' incredible visit. Quickly, I called my brother, Pastor Chola, and we marveled at what had happened.

After this incident, Mungai saw the two angels several times. Once, they were at the gate guarding and keeping watch. Then Gabriel left Angel Michael at the gate with his sword and proceeded to enter my son's room through the window.

"Mum, it was like magic! Angel Gabriel passed through the window. His body looked like it was cutting into small pieces. Then the pieces joined on the other side of the window."

Mungai attempted to vividly describe this event to me. I was completely puzzled. Twice, the angels were in his room, next to his bed. Angel Gabriel was at the edge of the bed, while Angel Michael was at the right side of the bed.

On one of the days, Mungai's friend, Kibet, had come for a sleepover. I slept with the two boys on my bed that night because Kibet was unwell. In the morning, Mungai reported how Angel Michael had come that night and stood right next to Kibet while Angel Gabriel stood at the edge of the bed.

"Angel Gabriel knows our names! He called them out loudly as he looked at each one of us. 'Lydia, Mungai, and Kibet!'"

The fact that the angel knew each of us by name is very significant. The Bible records God's knowledge of each and every person's name in the book of Isaiah. "Listen to me, you islands; hear this, you distant nations: Before I was born the Lord called me; from my birth He has made mention of my name" (Isa. 49:1).

"After a while, the two angels left the room through the roof and at great speed," Mungai narrated.

At the time, I had not yet started keeping a diary of these experiences, but I remember Mungai giving a similar description of the angels as he had done the very first time.

What is going on in my young child's life? I thought.

But I was glad he was seeing the angels and nothing sinister. Indeed, angels do watch over us. "If you make the Most High your dwelling—even the LORD, who is my refuge—then no harm will befall you, no disaster will come near your tent. For He will command His angels concerning you to guard you in all your ways, they will lift you up in their hands, so that you will not strike your foot against a stone" (Ps. 91:9–11). "The angel of the LORD encamps all around those who fear Him and He delivers them" (Ps. 34:7).

About Angels

According to what we read in the Bible, God created angels before the creation of the world and they were worshipping Him even then.

Where were you when I laid the earth's foundation? Tell, me if you understand. Who marked off its dimensions? Surely you know! Who stretched a measuring line across it? On what were its footings set or who laid its cornerstone—while the morning stars sang together and all the angels shouted for joy? (Job 38:4–7).

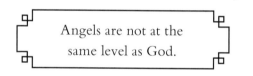

Angels are not at the same level as God.

Angels are spiritual beings who do not possess a physical body. The Bible describes them as ministering spirits. "Are not all angels ministering spirits sent to serve those who will inherit salvation?" (Heb. 1:14).

They are believed to be winged and very beautiful. Ezekiel saw visions of angels who had wings. The cherubim are a type of angel that guards God's holiness from defilement or sin. We read in the Bible that our 'Lord Almighty is enthroned between the cherubim.' (I Sam 4:4).The seraphim are another class of angels whose function is to praise God in heaven. They have six wings, two pairs cover their faces and feet while one pair is used for flying. They cover their faces because of the brilliance of God's glory. The Bible speaks of another type of angels known as 'archangels.' There are three of these angels namely Michael, Gabriel and Lucifer. Michael is always depicted to be in a spiritual conflict with Lucifer and his evil angels. Michael appears to be the commander of angels who do warfare for God. Gabriel on the other hand, plays a significant role in the Bible. He is always related with a mission of announcing God's messages to His people. Lucifer is the archangel who fell and became Satan. He rebelled against God in heaven and was cast down. We will read more about the archangels in the later chapters of this book.

There are several myths believed around the world concerning angels. Some people believe human beings transform into angels when they die, while others believe we can pray to angels to answer our prayers. However, whereas angels are spiritual beings and, in some instances, can take up a human form in order to minister to God's people, they are not at the same level as God. In many Biblical accounts, angels appeared to God's people as men. For example, in Genesis 18 describes three men visiting Abraham. One of them was the 'Angel of the Lord' and the other two were angels appearing as men.

One of the main roles of angels is to worship and praise God in heaven. This is because God created everything for His glory.

Another of their roles is to minister to God's people. We see several instances in the Bible where God sent His angels to minister to His people. Angels bring answers to the prayers of God's people. In the book of Daniel, God sent angels to shut the mouths of hungry lions so they would not make a meal out of Daniel.

Daniel 3 records the story of Daniel's friends, three Hebrew boys named Shadrach, Meshach, and Abednego, who an angel protected when King Nebuchadnezzar ordered his men to throw them into a burning fiery furnace. Ironically, the fire from the furnace burned up these men. No harm was caused to the three Hebrew boys. Interestingly, they did not even smell of smoke after they came out of the furnace.

In the New Testament, we read how an angel of the Lord opened prison doors for the apostle Peter so he could escape and continue to preach the word of God. "Suddenly an angel of the Lord appeared and a light shone in the cell. He struck Peter on the side and woke him up. 'Quick, get up!' he said, and the chains fell off Peter's wrists" (Acts 12:7).

Angels are also involved in battle on behalf of God's people because they are constantly fighting Satan and his demons. A description of how angels fight for us was earlier explained from the passage in Daniel 10:13–21.

The will of all angels is in line with the will of God. The angels of God rejoice in heaven when we repent of our sins and turn to Christ for salvation. Indeed, it is God's will that all men should be saved. "In the same way, I tell you, there is rejoicing in the presence of the angels of God over one sinner who repents" (Luke 15:10).

It is normal and common today to have angelic visits. Many Christians have claimed these glorious beings have visited them. Throughout the Bible, there are stories of individuals who were paid a visit by God's angels. The first appearance of angels is in the book of Genesis when Adam and Eve were sent away from the Garden of Eden. God sent two angels to guard the entrance to the garden with flaming swords. "After He drove the man out, He placed on the east side of the Garden of Eden cherubim and a flaming sword flashing back and forth to guard the way to the tree of life" (Gen. 3:24).

Other biblical personalities—Hagar, Jacob, Mary, Joseph, Zechariah, Paul, and among others—all had encounters with angels. If God allowed angels to visit people of old, there is no reason why angels cannot visit people in this age and time. God never changes. He is the same yesterday, today, and forever. "Jesus Christ is the same yesterday and today and forever" (Heb. 13:8).

Jesus Visits Mungai

After these encounters with the angels, Jesus visited Mungai in person. This was just before his seventh birthday. On October 16, 2009, I had just returned from an eleven-day work trip to Malawi. When the taxi pulled up in front of our house, I heard my son literally screaming with joy at the return of his mother. I was equally thrilled to see him because I had missed him so dearly.

While I was in the house trying to settle in and find out what had been going on while I was away, my son told me, "Mum, Jesus spoke to me today while in school."

"How did this happen?" I asked.

"Jesus spoke to me in my heart." He said this while touching his heart.

"What exactly did Jesus tell you?"

"Jesus said, 'Mungai, I am coming to visit you. I want you to see me.'" Mungai responded confidently.

By this time, my heart was beating with shock, excitement, and wonder, all the three emotions mixed together.

"When did the Lord speak to you?" I enquired.

He answered, "It happened while I was in the classroom."

"What were you doing when He spoke to you in your heart?" I continued with the questioning.

"I was not doing anything. I had finished my work. I was just seated in class, and then Jesus whispered to me in my heart."

I was surprised but excited at the same time. At this time, I did not know that this was just the beginning of a series of visitations by our precious Lord Jesus Christ, the King of kings and Lord of lords.

On the morning of October 20, 2009, just before 11:00, we were at home observing a public holiday then called Kenyatta Day, a day when the founding father of the nation of Kenya was celebrated. We began preparing ourselves to visit Mungai's grandparents in South B, a residential area in Nairobi.

As soon as we had finished showering and were getting ready, Mungai told me, "Mum, Jesus was here at night." He pointed next to his white chest of drawers. "Jesus had stood next to it. And Angel Michael was there near the door of my room. Angel Michael was carrying his sword, the one that has fire."

I was stunned at what he said, but I quickly remembered that Jesus had promised to come and visit this young son of mine just three days ago. Joy and awe filled me.

"How does Jesus look like?" I asked curiously.

"He is shinning white, His eyes are shining, His face is shining and His hair is white and shines too."

"You don't know?" he asked.

I smiled, not knowing what to respond. My son was surprised that I did not know what Jesus looked like and I had never really thought about it until now. My image of the Christ was from the photos I had seen of 'Him' hanging in people's homes and in shops.

"What was Jesus wearing?" I wanted to know so that I could picture Him in my mind.

"He wore something long and shining white. It looked like a dress, but it was not a dress, and it was long."

"How did you know it was Angel Michael at the door?"

"Angels do not change their clothes. They put on the same clothes every time, and they look the same. Their faces do not change."

I giggled.

> "Mum, Jesus spoke to me in school today. He spoke to me here in my heart. He said, 'I am going to visit you. I want you to see me.'"

A few days later, Mungai could still remember this visit by Jesus.

"Everything was shining when Jesus was in my room. Mum, all these books here, the toys, dinosaurs, and the teddy bear on top of this white chest drawer, they were all shining because of Jesus."

Amazingly, my son's description of Jesus matches the one recorded in the book of Revelation, as John, one of the twelve disciples of Jesus Christ, wrote.

"I turned around to see the voice that was speaking to me. And when I turned I saw seven golden lamp stands, and among the lamp stands was someone "like a son of man" dressed in a robe reaching down His feet and with a golden sash around His chest. His head and hair were white like wool, as white as snow and His eyes were like blazing fire" (Rev. 1:12–14).

Chapter 2

Mungai's First Visit to Heaven

On one of the evenings, Mungai and I were seated at the dining table at around five in the evening, just about to start on his homework.

Mungai started doing his homework and then paused. "Mum, today Jesus talked to me in school again."

I was very surprised but tried not to show it. I asked, "How did Jesus talk to you?"

"Jesus talked to me in my heart."

I probed further, "What were you doing when Jesus spoke to you?"

"Jesus whispered in my heart.
He said, 'Mungai, I am going to
show you heaven. I am going to show
you the gold in heaven.'"

He replied, "During lunch break, while I was playing and running around the school with my friends, I heard Jesus talking to me."

"It was like a whisper."

I asked, "What did Jesus say to you?"

"Jesus whispered in my heart, and He said, 'Mungai, I am going to show you heaven. I am going to show you the gold in heaven.'"

As stunned as I was to hear this, I totally believed him because he could not possibly have made up something like this.

Then he continued, "Something else happened but I do not want to share it with you."

I wondered why the hesitation and asked, "Why don't you want to tell me?"

"Because sometimes I feel like you don't believe me when I tell you some things."

I felt really rebuked. "Please forgive me."

"Please… tell me the rest of the story." I pleaded. I thank God that he is a forgiving child, so he agreed to tell it all.

"I was running and playing after Jesus had finished talking to me when I saw Angel Gabriel at the entry of the school gate."

"Angel Gabriel is so big, Mum. He is taller than the gate. I tried to peep at the guard at the gate to see whether he could see the angel, but I don't think the guard could see the angel. Then I called my friend and asked if he could see the angel at the gate, and he said no. But Mum, I could see Angel Gabriel, and I ran very close to him. He just stood there, and he was looking down at me."

"Did the angel say anything to you?"

"No, he did not say anything to me. After a short while, he disappeared. He just disappeared. I could not see him anymore."

At this juncture, I realized the Lord had been deliberately and purposefully leading me to understand supernatural experiences similar to the ones my son had been relating to me. For a period of time, I had been reading stories about eternity, heaven, angels, hell, and the demonic world. He was preparing me to understand that He and His Son Jesus Christ are real. I wondered what this visit to heaven would be like. I had never been to heaven, so I could not even imagine it. I stopped thinking about it. One thing for sure was that my son was going to experience heaven. The thought thrilled me beyond belief. I did not know when it was going to happen so I resolved in my heart to be patient and wait upon the Lord to do His will in my son's life.

> "Jesus said, 'Mungai, that one there next to the sun is Mercury, followed by Venus, and then planet Earth, where we have come from.'"

The following morning, Mungai woke up before me, and he was calling me to get up so as not to be late to school. The alarm had not yet gone off so I was trying to ignore him, persistently urging him to go back to sleep. This went on until he said something that made me sit up.

"Jesus came, and He took me to heaven," he said.

"What!" I woke up in a flash, causing all my sleep to disappear. I became totally alert from that moment.

What my son said to me that morning has changed my whole life. I will never ever be the same again. Mungai described how Jesus had come in that night through the roof. He pointed toward the roof of the bedroom, and my eyes followed his little finger as he pointed upwards.

He said, "Jesus came down and held my hand and we went up out through the roof."

"Mum, did you know that Jesus has a hole in His hand?"

"It is because Jesus had nails driven through His hands when He was crucified on the cross for our sins."

In the book of John, one of the disciples called Thomas had doubted that Jesus had been resurrected from the dead. Jesus asked Thomas to touch His hands and His side, which still bore the scars that showed the suffering He had endured for our salvation.

Quickly I asked Mungai, "How did you get to heaven?"

"As we were going up, I started to see the moon, then the sun and all the planets."

"Jesus began to show me all the planets and telling me their names! Jesus said, 'Mungai, that one there next to the sun is Mercury, followed by Venus, and then planet Earth, where we have come from.'" My son paused. "Mum, Jesus knows all the planets. He told me all the names of the planets: Mars, Jupiter, Saturn, Uranus, Neptune, and Pluto."

"Jesus knows them because He made them."

He exclaimed with joy. My son really loves the planets, so this was a real treat from Our Lord Jesus. At the time, though Mungai knew the planets, it was because I had taught him. They had not yet learned about them in school.

Mungai narrated, "We continued to fly up and up until we could not see the planets anymore. Then we entered heaven. I don't know whether we entered through a door, window or gate. We just flew in like this." He demonstrated by making a wave-like motion with his hands and making a rapid wind like sound."

"How did you know you were in heaven?"

"God was there. God is inside a lot of light, and He was looking at me. I did not see His face, but I know He was looking at me.

Then He walked towards me. Then He stopped and continued to look at me." Sounding very perplexed, Mungai said, "Mum, God was really looking at me."

"Did God say anything?"

"He did not say anything to me."

My heart was pounding. This was too much to take in. My son was in heaven? God had moved towards my son? He must have a really big plan for his life, his dad's, mine, and the whole world at large. I paused for a while.

"Did you see anything else in heaven?"

"Yes, many angels singing to God. Heaven shines. It is made out of gold."

That was all I could get out of my six-year-old.

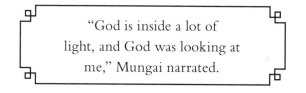

"God is inside a lot of
light, and God was looking at
me," Mungai narrated.

"How did you get back to bed?"

"Jesus brought me back."

He was giggling as he narrated, "Jesus was holding my hand and we flew back so fast that I did not see any planets. We entered the bedroom through the window and Jesus gently placed me on the bed and covered me. 'Good-bye Mungai' Jesus said to me and he left through the window."

On the following Sunday night, the pajamas Mungai was wearing when he first went to heaven were put on his bed for him to change into. He just kept staring at them. I went to my room and came back to his, and he was still staring.

"What's wrong?"

"These are the pajamas I was wearing when I went to heaven, and they were shining in heaven. They were shining so much because of the light that was coming from God. God shines so much that He makes the whole of heaven shine. It is God who makes heaven shine and not so much the gold."

A lot of information was coming out of a small child. God is clothed in light. The Bible says so. But how could Mungai have known this unless he was in heaven? He had definitely seen the One who sits on the throne in heaven. How else would he have known that God is inside light?

"Praise the Lord, O my soul. O Lord my God, You are very great; You are clothed with splendor and majesty. He wraps Himself with light as with a garment" (Ps. 104:1–3). "The city does not need the sun or the moon to shine on it, for the glory of God gives it light, and the Lamb is its lamp" (Rev. 21:23).

Jesus Promises to Visit Mungai on Saturday

On the evening of October 28, 2009, just before we commenced on his homework, Mungai reported that Jesus had appeared at the gate at school while they were having physical education.

"Did Jesus tell you anything?"

"No, He did not say anything to me. He just stood there, and He was looking at me. I don't think the other children at school could see Jesus."

That same evening, just as we were about to finish dinner, Mungai asked me, "Did you hear Jesus talking to me?"

Obviously perplexed, I responded, "I didn't hear anything."

He said, "Jesus just whispered to me, 'Mungai, I am coming on Saturday. I am going to show you the planets and heaven again.'" Immediately, my son looked at me with a very serious face. "When Jesus says He is going to do something, He does it!"

I believed him. I was happy that he had already figured out that God never lies. God is truth.

The following day at work, I told all my close friends that the Lord had promised to come visit my son that coming Saturday. The Lord had made a specific date with Mungai.

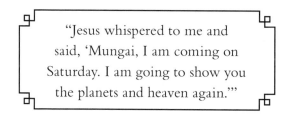

"Jesus whispered to me and said, 'Mungai, I am coming on Saturday. I am going to show you the planets and heaven again.'"

About Heaven

Heaven is a real place described in the Bible. It is believed to be upward because Jesus ascended upward into heaven after His resurrection. In Mark 16:19, it is recorded that Jesus was taken up into heaven and He sat at the right hand of God. In the book of Acts, Stephen was one of Christ's followers who was stoned to death. "'Look,' he said, 'I see heaven open and the Son of Man standing at the right hand of God'" (Acts 7:56).

Heaven is beyond the earth's airspace and beyond the stars and the planets. Paul, one of the apostles in the New Testament, talks about a third heaven.

I know a man in Christ who fourteen years ago was caught up to the third heaven. Whether it was in the body or out of the body I do not know—God knows. And I know that this man—whether in the body or apart from the body I do not know. But God knows was caught up to paradise. He heard inexpressible things, things that man is not permitted to tell (2 Cor. 12:2–3).

The Bible uses many names to refer to heaven: the kingdom of God (Eph. 5:5), the Father's house (John 14:2), a heavenly country (Heb. 11:16), the place of rest (Heb. 4:9 and Rev. 14:13), and paradise (2 Cor. 12:3–4). It is also referred to as a barn (Matt. 3:12). In 2 Peter1:11, it is referred to as the eternal kingdom.[1]

Once Mungai told me something very profound and very much in line with God's Word.

He said, "Mum, Jesus is the gate to heaven. You cannot go over Him, around Him, or under Him, but you have to go through Him in order to enter heaven!"

The Bible confirms this. "Jesus answered, 'I am the way and the truth and the life. No one comes to the Father except through me'" (John 14:6). Only through Jesus can one get to enter heaven. God sent His only son Jesus to die for us because He is holy and He cannot stand sin. The blood that Jesus shed on the cross washes away all sin. So if you believe in Him, you will have a ticket to heaven. You will be able to get to the Holy Father because your sins will be blotted away.

I continued to wait eagerly for Jesus' date with Mungai.

The Calling

On the Saturday that Jesus was to visit Mungai, my mother had come to visit us, so we were having a good time sharing and fellowshipping in my living room. I was telling her about the incredible things that the Lord was doing in our lives through our little son Mungai. My mother is involved in church ministry, so she was telling me about her ministry and how the Lord had helped her in difficult situations. As I sat there listening to her, I found my thoughts drifting away, wondering whether Jesus would visit my son that night.

---

1   Liardon, *We Saw Heaven*, 2000.

I thought to myself, *Lord, if you do not come, this whole story will be a sham.*

I had already told all my close colleagues at work that Jesus had promised to visit on Saturday. While I sat there doubting, my son, who was playing upstairs, came down. He positioned himself next to me, and he was playing with one of his toy cars. I could hear him saying "vroom" as he rolled his car along the arm of our yellow couch.

After about five to ten minutes, he said, "Jesus has just spoken to me right now. He has said, 'Mungai, I am coming tonight as I promised. I am going to show you the planets. I will even let you touch the stars, and I will take you to heaven.'"

I thought, almost aloud, *Was the Lord talking to me?*

My son could not have read my mind. All doubt left me instantly. Yes, the Lord knows all our thoughts. I quietly asked Jesus to forgive me. The sweet fellowship among my mum, our sweet Jesus, and me continued. "There hath not failed one word of all His good promise" (1 Kings 8:56b).

After about an hour, Mungai came down to us again. We had just finished lunch, and we were still seated at the dining area.

He said, "Mum, Jesus has just talked to me again and in a loud voice. He said, 'Mungai you are going to preach in Kenya and in the whole world so people can know and worship me, Jesus Christ.'"

That sentence was a mouthful for this seven-year-old as he tried to quickly spill out what our Lord had told him. My mum and I were so surprised, but we began rejoicing and thanking God for what He was going to do in Mungai's life. We thereafter prayed for him.

> "He said, 'Mungai, you are going to preach in Kenya and in the whole world so people can know and worship me, Jesus Christ.'"

Mungai and Mnjala in Heaven Together

Just as He had promised him on the Wednesday and as He had confirmed on the Saturday during my mother's visit, Jesus came. When we woke up on Sunday morning, Mungai explained excitedly, "Angel Gabriel and Angel Michael were here in the room at night." I was sleeping with Mungai in my bed because his father was away.

"Angel Gabriel stood by the door while Angel Michael stood next to you by your wardrobe. Then Angel Michael moved his hand in a waving motion and your wardrobe opened. I could see all your clothes and they were all shining brilliantly."

"The white clothes were shining even more," Mungai narrated to me, his puzzled-looking mother.

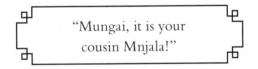

> "Mungai, it is your cousin Mnjala!"

"Mum, Jesus came and picked me from our bed and we left through the roof. We flew up very fast, it was as if we had wings."

"While we were in the air, I noticed another boy on Jesus' left hand. I could not see very well who it was because we were both shining so much because of the light that was coming from Jesus."

"Jesus, who is this boy?"

"Mungai, it is your cousin, Mnjala!"

"Mum, I was so happy to see my cousin. Mnjala was also so glad to see me. We laughed."

"So we continued upward toward the planets, and Jesus showed us all the planets, including dwarf planets." Mungai explained to me that Jesus told them that Pluto and 2003UB313 are dwarf planets. He fumbled to get these numbers out of his mouth while I searched on the Internet to find this planet that I had never heard of before. Eureka! I found it! This planet with many numbers is also known as Eris. I read that it was first discovered in January 2005. This planet does exist! It was discovered to be approximately 27 percent more massive than planet Pluto. The decision to demote Pluto from a fully fledged planet to a dwarf planet was made after the discovery of Eris.

The Bible states that God created everything, and not surprisingly, He showed the boys a new planet that He created billions of years ago, which scientists only discovered in 2005. I was in awe. The children had been shown a dwarf planet that I did not even know existed.

The Bible says, "In the beginning God created the heavens and the earth" (Gen. 1:1).

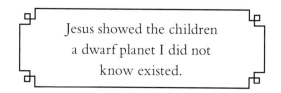

Jesus showed the children
a dwarf planet I did not
know existed.

"As we were viewing the planets, Angel Michael and Angel Gabriel, who had been left behind in the bedroom with you, flew up past us very fast like a bullet and went up to heaven." Mungai explained with amazement in his voice.

I thought, *No wonder I remember hearing myself giving praises to God like the psalmists while still in my sleep. I had sensed the presence of God with me as I slept.*

Jesus also allowed the children to touch the asteroids, which are large rocks and boulders hanging in the galaxy.

"They were so huge but we could push them with one finger and they would move because we were with Jesus. We had so much of fun!" Mungai said gleefully.

Chapter 3

God Speaks from His Throne

> God said, "Mungai and
> Mnjala, sit down."

After Jesus finished showing them the planets, they entered
heaven, and God made two golden chairs appear. These chairs
came out of nowhere, and God, without touching them, made
them move and placed them in front of the children. Mungai
seemed much taken up by God's power to make something appear
out of nowhere.

He asked me, "How does God do that?"

I explained, "God is all powerful, so He is able to do
anything."

Mungai said, "God asked us to sit in one chair."

God said, "Mungai and Mnjala, sit down."

Mungai said, "But God, the chair is too small."

God told him, "Just sit down. You will fit."

Sure enough, when they sat down, they both fit perfectly into the golden chair.

Mungai said, "The chair expanded so we were both able to fit."

I felt as though God was teaching them to trust in Him.

Then God began to talk to them about the human back.

Mungai paused. "God's voice is so big, but someone cannot feel afraid when He is talking. God's voice is bigger than in the movie of Moses that we watch here."

"God said, 'The back is a very important part of the body and it helps us lift ourselves up when we are lying down. Some bones in the back will cause one not be able to walk if he is injured.'"

Mungai paused. "Mum, is it true that it could affect one's ability to walk if the back were injured?"

"It is true. It is a state called paralysis."

"After God taught us about the back, he asked us to sit where everybody else was. He told us to sit next to Moses. People were seated like in a church congregation. Jesus was at the front holding a very big golden Bible, and he was reading from the book of Mathew. Jesus told us that he loves little children very much."

Then little children were brought to Jesus for Him to place His hands on them and pray for them. But the disciples rebuked those who brought them. "Jesus said, 'Let the little children come to me, and do not hinder them, for the kingdom of heaven belongs to such as these'" (Matt. 19:13–14).

The two boys sat together again on the same chair, a golden chair, and they sat next to Moses. Others in the crowd were: Mary and Joseph, Mary, the mother of John; Simon Peter; John the Baptist; David; Sarah; and Abraham. They were able to recognize everyone when they saw him or her because God put this knowledge in their hearts.

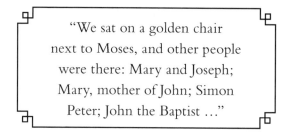

"We sat on a golden chair next to Moses, and other people were there: Mary and Joseph; Mary, mother of John; Simon Peter; John the Baptist …"

After this, the Lord started singing, "Jesus loves the little children, all the children of the world, red and yellow, black and white, they are precious in His sight. Jesus loves the little children of the world."

Mungai paused. "Mum, can you sing this song for me?"

I did. My voice was choking because I could not imagine what the Lord had just done to me through my son. I knew from that moment that I would never be the same again. My life took on a new meaning and perspective. I had felt the touch of God. I knew beyond the shadow of a doubt that heaven exists, that it is not just another story in the Bible or the "pie in the sky" theory, as some scholars describe it to be. It is real!

Mungai lay on my chest as I sang to him. It was a very intense moment. Jesus had touched us.

He said, "While we were still in heaven, Jesus told us that He was coming down to earth to heal sick people."

The boys were left in heaven singing. After a while, Jesus returned and took the boys to see the planets again. He allowed them to touch the stars just as He had promised Mungai. Thereafter, Jesus held Mungai's hand and brought him back to bed, covered him, told him good night, and left through the window.

Jesus also dropped off Mnjala in his bedroom. Jesus is omnipresent, so He can be in many places at the same time.

A Day with Jesus

That Sunday morning, I was extremely thrilled as Mungai narrated this awesome story to me. I had expected Our Lord Jesus to visit just as He had promised, but I never expected such an incredible visitation. I had never in my wildest dreams thought that my son and my nephew would be visited and taken to heaven at the same time. I had sensed the presence of God so strongly in our room that night and sang praises to Him. I took the phone and called my mum, and we were just praising our God for that awesome work that He was doing in our lives. I thereafter called my sister Janet, Mnjala's mother, and confirmed that Mnjala had told her the exact same story.

My sister was laughing very hard. "My son knows all the planets, yet no one ever taught him!"

I asked to talk to him, and he repeated the same experience in heaven as Mungai had described to me. We were so awed. Janet was so surprised that her son now knew the planets. He was just babbling them out one by one. He had learned them from the one who created them.

We agreed to meet in town later that morning and go to church together. We had a wonderful service at Destiny Chapel, a church that my brother Chola and three other pastors had just planted. We wanted to visit and support them for a couple Sundays.

On our way back home from church, the two children told us incredible things. It was as though God had opened their spiritual eyes and they could see into the supernatural. They said Jesus and Angel Gabriel were in the car with us.

"It is like Mungai is sitting on Jesus, and I am seated on Angel Gabriel," Mnjala explained.

Then they would say things like, "There is an angel on that building!"

As we approached a roundabout, Mungai exclaimed, "An angel just stopped that truck, Mum! It was coming toward you too fast!"

So I asked them, "Can you ask Jesus if I am driving on the correct side of the road?"

They both said, "He said yes!"

We got home and had lunch. The boys ate quickly so they could play. They went into the computer room where we keep the toys.

After a while, Mungai came running to me. "Mum, Jesus is here with us."

My sister and I ran into the computer room, but we could not see anything.

I asked, "Is Jesus alone?"

Mungai replied, "Jesus is here with Angel Gabriel. Angel Michael was here, too, but Jesus has told us that he has gone to fight."

So we started asking questions.

My sister Janet asked, "Please ask Jesus if we could see Him also?"

"Not now." Jesus replied through the children.

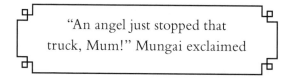

"An angel just stopped that truck, Mum!" Mungai exclaimed

I told Mungai that he could ask Jesus for anything he wanted.

"Jesus, can you please help my mum get another job where she will not be travelling because I miss her so much when she is gone."

Jesus told him, "The answer is yes."

"Mungai, ask about your dad's salvation and his returning to church." I urged.

"Again, Jesus has said 'yes.'"

On our way home that day, we met our pastor, Pastor George Mathu, who jokingly asked Mungai to ask Jesus about our church when he saw Him next. I remembered that conversation, so I told Mungai to ask about the church.

In a cute, little voice, Mungai said, "Jesus, tell me about Pastor George's church."

Honestly, the two kids looked as though they were talking to the wall.

Mungai reported, "Jesus has said, 'In that church, I am praised, and I am honored.'"

This was great news! I was so glad and could not wait to share it with the pastor and our congregation at Eagle's Faith Christian Centre.

Janet and I were, of course, very amazed. We returned to the dining table to continue planning for the birthday party for the two boys. After a short while, Mungai came to me, pulled me into the computer room, and said we needed to go and pray where Jesus was. So we entered the computer room where the children had been playing.

I went on my knees. "Where is Jesus standing?"

They both pointed. Then they said, "He is with Angel Gabriel."

I asked Mungai to pray first, and he prayed for their birthday party. Next, it was my turn to pray, and this whole experience extremely overwhelmed me. Later, I will share how God answered our prayers.

When we were about to leave the house, the children kept telling us where Jesus was. It seemed as though He would appear at different corners of the house at the same time. I was getting water from the fridge, and my son would exclaim that Jesus was in the kitchen. Then He was in the living room, thereafter at the door, and then in my car. It is difficult to put in words exactly what was taking place in our home that evening. Jesus is indeed omnipresent.

We left the house and dropped our visitors at the bus stop. Mungai and I proceeded to a Chinese restaurant to get some takeaway dinner. As we were leaving the restaurant, Mungai told me that Jesus was appearing in front of him, behind him, on the left side, and on the right side. How awesome!

Jesus Confirms That the Bible Is His Word

On November 3, 2009, as I was putting Mungai to bed, I picked up his Children's Bible. I was just about to read it to him when he spoke.

"Jesus is present in the room with us." He nudged me. "Jesus is right there next to the floor lamp."

I felt a little overwhelmed to imagine that the Lord Jesus, the King of kings and Lord of lords, was right there with us. He had chosen to visit us. We were not special in any way, just regular people trying to go about our normal day-to-day affairs. This was our usual time for Bible stories, and Jesus showed up.

I asked Mungai, "Can you ask Jesus which story I should read for you?"

"Jesus can hear what you are asking. He has said, 'Tell your mum that she can read to you any story she likes because the whole Bible is about me.'"

"Mungai, you can ask Jesus for what you need."

"Jesus, can you help me pass my exams?"

"Mum, Jesus has told me, 'For as long as you do what I have instructed you to do, you will pass your exams.'"

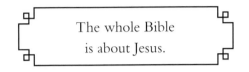

The whole Bible
is about Jesus.

The big lesson for me that evening was the fact that the Bible is God's Word and it doesn't matter which part of it we read so long as we read it.

This incident reminded me of a story about my grandfather, Ibrahim Chola, who loved to read the Bible. He would carry his Bible to the field and read it while his cows were grazing. He would sit under a tree and carefully study the word of God. One day, he lost his spectacles in the field, and he was so sad because he could not read without them. He searched all over for them but in vain. He simply could not trace them in the thick grass.

On the third day, feeling very frustrated about his lost spectacles, he sat under a tree to rest. After a while, one of his favorite cows came over to him, holding the spectacles in its mouth. The cow had found the spectacles and handed them over to their rightful owner! The cow just walked close to my grandfather and dropped the spectacles next to him. He was very pleased but completely amazed at how the cow had found and brought back his spectacles to him so he could continue to read his precious Bible.

I am sure the Lord had a hand in this. He wants us to read His Word every day because that is one of the ways He is able to talk to us. Read yours, and you will be able to respond to the person who speaks to us in the Bible, God.

My grandfather loved Jesus with all his heart, and he taught his children to love God. He was not a very wealthy man so he did not have much in terms of an inheritance to leave behind for his children, but he left them with the most precious thing in the world, the knowledge of the salvation of our Lord Jesus. He built his treasure where it matters most, in heaven where moth and rust do not destroy. Sometimes I picture him up in heaven, excited that his great-grandchildren, Mungai and Mnjala, are visitors to heaven.

About the Bible

The word "Bible" comes from the Greek "biblia," the word for "the books." Wycliffe made up the English word when he translated it into English in the fifteenth century. The Bible is the source of the Christian religion in that it contains the words spoken by God and how the Christian is to apply His words to his or her daily life.

The Bible is a collection of sixty-six books. The sixty-six books are divided into two parts: thirty-nine books in the Old Testament and twenty-seven books in the New Testament. The Old Testament covers a sweep of history, from the creation of the world to about 400 BC. Its books include poetry, history, prophecy and law, proverbs, parables, narratives, and songs. They all tell the story of God's troubled relationship with His people. Basically, it describes the origin of man in the Garden of Eden, along with his fall into sin and out of fellowship with God. Then God called out a special people called the Israelites. He promised them a future Messiah who would restore mankind's relationship with God. This Messiah is Jesus Christ, whose life is the center of the New Testament. He was born of a virgin called Mary. He lived on earth and taught His people about Himself. Then he was crucified, died on the cross, and rose again on the third day. Death is the penalty He paid for our sins so all mankind could be reconciled to God.

The New Testament covers the amazing life of Jesus Christ Our Lord, the birth of the Church, and the prophecies of the tribulations and the end-times. The New Testament contains four accounts of Jesus' life called the Gospels that his disciples wrote: Matthew, Mark, Luke, and John. In the book of Acts are the stories of how Jesus' followers spread His message around the world. Letters or epistles to Christians follow, many written from prison cells by Jesus' followers like Paul, Peter, James, and John. Finally, there is a prediction about the end of the world and the start of a new world after God's judgment is complete.

> When we are facing life's challenges like when we are in pain or lack, suffering, mourning, downcast, or discouraged, we find strength in the word of God.

The books of the Bible were written over a period of about sixteen hundred years and under the inspiration of the Holy Spirit. Over forty authors, ranging from farmers, kings, poets, historians, prophets, warriors, priests, fishermen, kings, philosophers, and even shepherds, wrote it. Despite this diversity of authorship, the books of the Bible show a common understanding and a unified teaching running right through. The Old Testament is believed to have been written from the twelfth to the second century BC and was written in classical Hebrew. The New Testament centers on the life of Jesus and was written from about 50 AD to about 95 AD. It is the fulfillment of the Old Testament prophecies. The Bible was written in three languages: Hebrew, Aramaic, and Koine Greek.

The Bible is an anchor to life's journey. It reveals God to us in the stories contained in it. It directs us to Jesus, who is God. We get to understand who God is and how He loves all His people.

We get to read how God sacrificially gave Jesus Christ, His one and only son, in order to restore His people back to Himself.

The Bible also gives guidance for living a good and fulfilled life here on earth. We find high standards for conduct, guidelines for knowing right from wrong, and principles to help us in this world. It is a refuge in times of trouble. When we are facing life's challenges, like when we are in pain or lack, suffering, mourning, downcast, or discouraged, we find strength in the word of God.

The Bible provides insight regarding who we are in God. We were created for a reason, a purpose, and a destiny, and the Bible reveals this to us. Life has more meaning as we get to understand God's will for us, that He created us, He loves us, and He has a good plan for our future.

The Bible is also a storehouse of beautiful stories that reveal God's power, strength, and might. We get to read the miraculous signs and wonders that He who created us performed. Remember the story of Daniel in the lion's den? Noah and the ark? Jonah in the whale's stomach? Joseph's coat of many colors? The ten plagues in Egypt? The parting of the Red Sea? Shadrach, Meshach, and Abednego in the fiery furnace? Jesus' parables and miracles? In these stories, we recognize the victories and failures of ordinary people. We get to learn from their trials and use them to encourage ourselves. When I was growing up, I enjoyed reading these stories. They are amazing stories about God Almighty.

Jesus explained that the Bible is a testimony of Himself. "You diligently study the Scriptures because you think that by them you possess eternal life. These are the Scriptures that testify about me, you refuse to come to me to have life" (John 5:39).

The Bible is the bestselling book in history because it is about God and His love for His creation. In as much as different authors wrote it, God inspired them all. "All Scripture is God-breathed, and it is useful for teaching, rebuking, correcting and training in righteousness" (2 Tim. 3:16).

This means the Bible comes directly from God. There are no mistakes in its writings. It addresses all life's situations and gives solutions. If you do not have a Bible, please get a copy today!

Chapter 4

Jesus Listens When We Pray

As I was driving Mungai to school one day, I began to pray for him. He was going to sit for his exams, so I told him that we were going to pray for him and the day and to thank God for protecting us through the night. I began the prayer with "Dear Jesus" and finished it with "It is in Jesus' most precious name that we pray and believe in. Amen."

As soon as I finished praying, Mungai touched my lap. "Mum, as soon as you said 'Dear Jesus,' He appeared in the backseat of the car. He was listening to your prayer. He left as soon as you said the word 'Amen.'"

That was a big lesson right there, and it changed the way I perceive prayer from that day forward. I have started to talk to God more, knowing He is actually there listening to me. And because He listens, He definitely answers. Even when He does not answer instantly, He will answer at the best and most appropriate time. This is a lesson not just for me but for all of us. Jesus wants us to know that He listens when we pray.

About Prayer

Jesus taught His disciples how to pray. Prayer is important because it is the means of talking to God our Father. "He said to them, 'When you pray say: Father, hallowed be your name, your kingdom come. Give us each day our daily bread. Forgive us our sins, for we also forgive everyone who sins against us. And lead us not into temptation'" (Luke 11:2–4).

Prayer is simply talking to God. It is having a conversation with our Maker who is in heaven. Those who believe in Christ Jesus should pray from their hearts and in their own words at any time of the day or night. We need not try to impress God with big words or impressive language. There is no right or wrong position for prayer. One can pray standing, kneeling, seated, walking, or with his or her eyes open or closed. What is important is that you tell God what is in your heart and you listen to your heart to hear from Him.

Prayer is not only a way to communicate with our God, but it also develops our relationship with Him. The same way we develop our earthly relationships with each other through communication, so it is with God. Through prayer, we are able to speak to God, and He is also able to speak to us. We became more intimate with God as we continue to fellowship with Him through prayer.

> *And when you pray, do not keep on babbling like pagans, for they think they will be heard because of their many words*
> Matthew 6:7

On many occasions, we feel as though we do not know how to pray. The secret is to tell God what you feel in your heart. He promised to send us a helper, who is His Holy Spirit to direct, counsel, and teach us. "In the same way, the Spirit helps us in our weaknesses. We do not know what we ought to pray for, but the Spirit Himself intercedes for us with groans that words cannot express" (Rom. 8:26).

When you rely on the Holy Spirit to assist you in prayer, He will search your heart and intercede for you in accordance to the will of God. You need not read prayers from a book; just express yourself as though you are talking to a good friend or to your father or mother. Above all, allow the Holy Spirit to direct you as you pray.

Many cares of this world cause us to be anxious, troubled, worried, and discouraged, but Jesus taught us to cast all our cares unto Him through prayer. We should therefore pray on all occasions when we have plenty or scarce, when we are joyful or sad, when we are well or unwell, or when we do or don't feel like it. "Do not be anxious about anything but in everything by prayer and petition with thanksgiving present your request to God. And the peace of God which transcends all understanding will guard your hearts and your minds in Christ Jesus" (Phil. 4:6-7).

Prayer is not only reserved for the pastors, evangelists, priests, church elders, or bishops, but it is for all who believe in Christ. We need to make a habit of praying every day from the bottom of our hearts in honesty and love toward God our Father. If you do not believe in Jesus, today you have a chance to do so. Ask Him in prayer to be your Lord, and He will. Thereafter, start reading your Bible and praying every day. Moreover, involve yourself with other Bible-believing Christians so they can direct you in the ways of the Lord.

Uncle Ken Is in Heaven

I had travelled to Ethiopia for work. This time round, I was in Addis Ababa for a night and then left for Axum the following day, which was a Saturday. Axum is about two hours away by air from Addis Ababa, the capital city of Ethiopia, but the flight can have stops at Gonder, Makele, or Lalibela. All this landing and taking off always made me feel very far away from home. I was already feeling homesick by the first day, so I called home to find out how everyone was doing. I also wanted to let them know that I was well and I had arrived safely. Afterwards, I relaxed and tried to focus on my work. The week went by very smoothly, and because I was very busy, it seemed to have gone by even faster.

At the end of the week, I called home again and spoke to Mungai. I was not expecting to hear what he was going to tell me. He had hardly greeted me. Then in an excited voice, he said, "I saw Uncle Ken in heaven. Mum, I saw Uncle Ken in heaven!"

Words cannot express the joy I felt in my heart to hear those words. This was very good news! I looked forward to returning home so I could get the full story. Calling from Axum is not cheap, and the connection is not very good most of the time, but I knew I had heard my son right. His words rang in my mind the whole week.

Uncle Ken is my husband's brother who had passed on in August 2008. He died at the age of forty six. He had been ill for a very long time. As he suffered on his deathbed, he accepted Jesus as his Lord and Savior. He had confirmed this to my mother-in-law just before he went into a coma. He had told her not to worry because he had made it right with God. Indeed, this is all it takes to make it to heaven. Making it right with God! I also spent a lot of time with him telling him about God and had bought him a Bible, which he treasured very much and made a point to read even when he was very ill.

I returned home from Ethiopia before the end of the second week. I spent the afternoon together with Mungai and his father. Mungai told me that Jesus had spent the whole night with them in our room, seated on a black seat that we have in my room.

Jesus then called out to Mungai, "Mungai!"

Mungai woke up and told Jesus, "I do not want my dad to go to hell. I want him to go to heaven."

And Jesus replied, "Okay, Mungai."

As I was unpacking my bags and organizing our home, Mungai told me that Jesus had promised to spend the whole of Christmas Day with us. Christmas was just a few weeks away so this was an exciting revelation.

I began to inquire about Uncle Ken. I needed to get a firsthand account of this experience directly from the horse's mouth. Mungai informed me that he had seen Uncle Ken twice in heaven. The first time, they did not say anything to each other, but when he saw him the second time round, he talked to Uncle Ken and asked him whether he still remembered us. Uncle Ken responded that he did remember home and all of us.

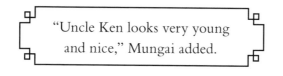

"Uncle Ken looks very young and nice," Mungai added.

Then Mungai told him that some people were not sure whether he had gone to heaven or hell. Mungai told him, now that he had seen him, he would tell everyone that he saw him in heaven. It was an interesting observation from my son because there was the general mood of apprehension in the family regarding where Ken had gone after death. The fact that Ken had waited up to almost the last minute before giving his life to the Lord was the reason. Many hoped he had made it, but they were not quite sure.

In Luke 23, the Bible records the story of two criminals who hung on the cross next to Jesus. One of the criminals hurled insults at Jesus, asking Him to save them and save Himself. The other recognized he was a sinner and requested Jesus to remember him when He went to His kingdom, to which Jesus replied that he would be with Him that very day in paradise. The latter received God's grace at the last minute of his life, just like Uncle Ken.

"Uncle Ken looks very young and nice," Mungai added as he ran off to get a toy.

The first time Mungai saw Uncle Ken in heaven, he was at his Uncle Kinuthia's house, and I was in Ethiopia. Kinuthia is my brother-in-law, and together with his wife Annie, they have two young children, Ryan and Trudy. Mungai had visited heaven on Saturday night. On Sunday morning, he woke up excitedly to tell his uncle and aunty the good news of what he had seen there. They later told me how amazed they were when they heard Mungai talking about heaven and what he saw.

Mungai narrated to me how Jesus and Angel Gabriel had spent the day with them. He told me that, at one time, Jesus was carrying Trudy on His lap as she played on the carpet with her doll.

His cousin Ryan kept asking after every ten minutes, "Are they still here with us?"

The children were very excited about the presence of Jesus and an angel with them. Mungai said that, after he shared this story with his uncle and aunt, he was so glad that they all believed him, all except their housekeeper who could not imagine such a thing.

Amazingly, Mnjala now knows Uncle Ken, yet they never met while he was alive here on earth. Mnjala said something very interesting to his mum the first time he saw Uncle Ken. He said, "Mum, Mungai has an uncle who lives in heaven."

Those Who Die in Christ Jesus Go to Heaven

The Bible records in several passages that those who die in Christ Jesus go to heaven. Our Lord Christ Jesus promised that He would prepare a place for us. This place is heaven. He promised that we would be where He is. He is at the right hand of God the Father.

> "In my Father's house are many rooms; if it were not so, I would not have told you. I am going there to prepare a place for you. And if I go and prepare a place for you, I will come back and take you to be with me that you also may be where I am. You know the way to the place where I am going." (John 14:2-4).

> "Enter through the narrow gate. For wide is the gate and broad is the road that leads to destruction, and many enter through it. But small is the gate and narrow the road that leads to life and only a few find it" (Matt. 7:13–14).

The road that leads to life is the road that leads to heaven. Life in this verse means eternal life. There is a gate that leads to God in heaven and another that leads to hell and destruction.

> *Jesus answered, 'I am the way and the truth and the life. No-one comes to the Father except through me.'*
> John 14:6

Paul, who was one of the apostles of Jesus in the New Testament, says that to die is gain because one will be in the presence of God in heaven. Death does not have a sting because the person who has departed has gone to be with God and shall be reunited with loved ones as long as he died in Christ Jesus. This is because Jesus is the gateway to heaven.

For those who believe in Jesus Christ, the Bible tells us that, after death, the believers' souls are taken to heaven because their sins have been forgiven by virtue of having received Christ as their Savior. For so long as we are still alive on this earth, we are away from the Lord. We are made of body, spirit, and soul. Paul is explaining that, when we are in this body, meaning that when we are alive on earth, we are away from God who is in heaven.

> "Therefore we are always confident and know that as long as we are at home in the body we are away from the Lord. We live by faith, not by sight. We are confident, I say, and would prefer to be away from the body and at home with the Lord" (2 Cor. 5:6–8).

> "I am torn between the two: I desire to depart and be with Christ which is better by far" (Phil. 1:23).

These passages in the Bible make a lot of sense to me as I remember how my son saw his uncle in heaven. It is by far better for him that he is with Christ in heaven even though we miss him here. He had suffered so much pain and sickness, but he is now well with the Lord. I thank God that he had made up with God before his death. "For God so loved the world that He gave His one and only Son, that whoever believes in Him shall not perish but have eternal life" (John 3:16).

In the above verse, the word "everlasting" means "eternal life." That is life that does not have an end. Our souls are eternal; they live forever. Those who believe in God will definitely live happily forever in heaven with Him.

Chapter 5

Pastor Chola's Story

Pastor Joel Chola is my dear brother, and he is one of the founders and associate pastors of Destiny Chapel located in Nairobi. His story is also amazing as it proves to us once again that we are made out of body, soul, and spirit and our spirits live on after we die. Pastor Chola has had what in scientific terms is known as "near death experience" or NDE. NDE, as described in layman's terms, is when a person has been declared clinically dead, so all the vitals, that is, the heartbeat, the pulse, and breathing, have come to a stop.

Wikipedia defines NDE as "a broad range of personal experiences associated with impending death, encompassing multiple possible sensations including detachment from the body; feelings of levitation; extreme fear; total serenity, security or warmth; the experience of absolute dissolution; and the presence of a light. These phenomena are usually reported after an individual has been pronounced clinically dead or otherwise very close to death, hence the term near death experience. With the recent developments in cardiac resuscitation techniques, the number of reported NDEs has increased. Many in the scientific community regard such experiences as hallucinatory while paranormal specialists and some mainstream scientists claim them to be evidence of an afterlife."

Now I agree with the mainstream scientist because my brother's story explains a bit of the afterlife and provides a lot of evidence that we indeed have a part of us that lives on. When we leave this body, we merely do not just disappear, leaving this body to rot in the grave. Neither do we go to another world to reincarnate into some different animal or form as some religions believe. Our spirits actually go to reside in heaven or hell, according to whether we accepted or rejected Jesus Christ, the Lord and King of this universe.

> He wanted to tell the doctor that he was okay because he felt well, but he realized they were not seeing or hearing him. They were looking down at his lifeless body and doing everything they could to get it to breathe and to get his heart pumping again.

My brother's NDE took place over the Easter weekend in 2001. He had just come home from surgery. He'd had his sinuses removed successfully, and he was recuperating at home. He had been at home for only two days since this surgery when he began to have nosebleeds. The first and second nosebleeds were not so bad, but the third and fourth brought a lot of concern to him and his wife Pauline. It was almost impossible to control the fourth nosebleed, so they made a quick decision to return to the hospital.

Upon their arrival at the hospital, one of his doctors attended to him and had to admit him in order to perform surgery. He stuffed his nose with gauzes and booked the theatre for early the following day. My brother had to return to the theatre for the doctor to cauterize what was causing the nosebleeds. After this first aid, the doctor left the hospital. He thought he had left him safe in the nurses' hands, but it turned out to be the worst night of his life. By three o'clock in the morning, the bleeding had started again, heavily soaking the gauzes. Pastor Chola desperately called out to the nurses, who quickly came to his aid, putting lots of ice and trying to apply as much pressure as they could. Somehow, they managed to control the bleeding.

However, by the next morning at seven o'clock, the bleeding pushed out the gauzes that the doctor had inserted. In a short while, the bleeding began all over again. My brother tried to stop it himself by applying pressure to his nose, but the blood gushed out through his mouth, his eyes, and every opening on his face. The nightmare that started that night was getting worse as the morning advanced. The nurses tried to reach the doctor but in vain.

My dear brother was weak, exhausted, worn out, and sleepy, but worst of all, he felt and knew that he was going to die. His wife and my father had been in to see him earlier that morning, but due to hospital policy, they could not stay long. They left to return home. He surrendered his cell phone to his wife for safe custody because he knew he was going to go into the theatre in a few moments, but he would regret this decision later on. He now needed a cell phone to call for help because he realized from the way his body was reacting that he was a dying man. So he tried to borrow one from the patient next to him. To show you how oblivious people are to death, the patient asked him which of the networks he wanted to make his call to. Here was a man dying, and instead of trying to assist him call his wife, he was concerned about how much it would cost him to call a different network.

Fortunately, another patient brought some sense to the situation. He said, "Just give him your phone. This could be his last call."

This fellow did not know how close to the truth he was. So my brother got the phone and quickly called his wife Pauline, asking her to pray for him and to alert all the pastors to pray for him. This request worried his wife. She knew in her heart and heard it in his voice that her husband's life was in grave danger. So she telephoned as many people as she could, and together with my mother, with whom she was with at the time, they prayed to God to spare his life. As Pastor Chola gave back the mobile phone, he looked at himself in a mirror that was right next to his bed. To his surprise, he saw blood coming out of his tear ducts. As he turned to sit back on his bed, one of his doctors happened to come by to check on him. Seeing his state and condition, she said he should be taken back to the operating theatre immediately.

This was just one of the miracles that is part of this story. The doctor, who had happened to come by his bed, was just doing her rounds, but she had decided to specifically come and check on him because he had attended their clinic. She had heard that he had been admitted the night before. A nurse came to wheel Pastor Chola into the operating room.

He told me later, "I felt that the nurse was too slow. He seemed to be taking his time, yet I felt I was in critical shape and urgently needed immediate medical attention."

He was still bleeding, but it seemed much less because he had lost a lot of blood. As the stretcher was being pushed into the theatre, my brother was praying and hanging in there. As he went past one of the doors that led to the theatre, a wonderful white woman met him there. We later came to discover that this woman was an American lady who felt God had called her to pray for people who found themselves in critical situations, like that of my brother.

She looked at the name tag on his wrist. "Pastor Chola, we heard there was an emergency coming. You can now stop praying. I will take over from here."

On hearing that, my brother gave in to an overwhelming urge he had been feeling, which was to put his head down and sleep. Little did he know that this urge was not sleep but death! He had been slowly dying because of blood loss, but he had been fighting death until that moment. Amazingly, at the moment he died, he did not even realize he was dead. He said he remembered seeing one of the nurses who was pushing the stretcher trying to wake him up by yelling and asking him not to sleep. He tried to talk to her to tell her he was all right, but she seemed not to hear him. He felt as though she was ignoring him. Then because of the hurry she was in, she slipped and fell and could no longer push the stretcher because she had sprained her wrist. She then ran aside and rang a bell to call for help. When she came back to Pastor Chola's side, he tried to talk to her again, but she still seemed not to hear him. By this time, he had been wheeled into the operating room, and everyone in there was going crazy.

Questions were flying around. "He has lost a lot of blood. What is his blood group? What procedure was done on him?"

My brother tried to talk to them, but just like the nurse, they seemed not to hear him or just ignored him. That's when my brother realized that he was no longer in his body. He seemed to be watching everything from a sitting position. He even saw the straight flat line on the monitoring machine. He could see his body lying on the hospital operating bed.

He could also hear the doctor saying in a panic, "We have no pulse. I cannot find his heartbeat, and he is not breathing."

He could hear all this while he was out of his body. He saw the doctor and the attendants working hard to resuscitate his body. He wanted to tell the doctor that he was all right because he felt well, but he realized they were not listening nor looking up at him. They were looking down at his lifeless body and doing everything they could to get it functioning and his heart pumping again.

Immediately, it hit him. *I must be dead*, he thought. At that moment, he thought about his wife and two children, Duncan and Ciru, but that's all it was, just a thought. *My poor wife and kids.* That's the strange thing about death. It doesn't disturb the dead as much as it does the living.

As he looked around, he saw a man looking at him. This man was dressed just like everyone else in the theatre, but he was making eye contact with him. The man looked at him and smiled, and my brother smiled back. At that moment, the man held my brother as you would a small child when putting him into bed and laid him back into his body. That's when my brother realized that this was an angel. They never made any conversation, and in a split second, the angel had put him back into his body. Instantly, all his vital organs began to function again. His heart started beating, he was breathing again, and he even responded to the doctor who had just inquired about his blood group.

"It is O positive. My blood group is O positive," my brother responded in a feeble voice.

He then grabbed the hand of one of the attendees who was pressing the oxygen mask too hard over his nose. He was alive again! They completed the surgery and discovered that one of the main arteries that had opened up was causing the bleeding.

Another miracle that took place, apart from the one of him coming back to his body, was that the doctors thought he would have to go to the Intensive Care Unit or High Dependency Unit because some of his vital organs could have failed because they had not had enough blood flow into them for a period of time. This was not to be the case because he was perfectly fine when he came back to his body. He was taken back to the regular ward. We normally joke and say that Pastor Chola came back with ten times more energy than he had before.

My brother's story, among many others, is evidence that we have a spirit that lives on after this body ceases to live.

About the Body, Spirit, and Soul

The Bible is clear that man is composed of three distinct parts: body, spirit, and soul. "May God Himself, the God of peace, sanctify you through and through. May your whole spirit, soul and body be kept blameless at the coming of our Lord Jesus Christ" (1 Thess. 5:2).

The physical body is organic, temporary, and ever-changing, and it is prone to sicknesses, disease, injury, aging, and death. The soul consists of emotions, the mind, and will. The spirit is the part of us that never dies. It is the part of us that is alive, yet we cannot see it. It is the part of us that speaks to God and hears from God. The spirit and soul move together as one and work together. Many people cannot differentiate the two. The spirit is the part of us that identifies with God, whereas the soul consists of emotions, the will, and mind. "The Lamp of the Lord searches the spirit of man, it searches out his inmost being" (Prov. 20:27).

The spirit is renewed and changed the minute a person accepts Jesus into his or her heart. God converts that individual because now the Holy Spirit of God starts to live within him or her. "But if Christ is in you, your body is dead because of sin, yet your spirit is alive because of righteousness" (Rom. 8:10).

The soul is changed gradually through daily devotion to God as one allows himself or herself to submit to the Lord Jesus and slowly dying to self and allowing the Holy Spirit through His presence and power to control his or her life.

When the Spirit of God changes our spirits, we begin to emit the fruit of the Holy Spirit, which are love, joy, peace, kindness, honesty, self-control, righteousness, patience, and goodness. The fact we have a spirit and God is Spirit, He is able to speak to us. He speaks to us through His Word, the Bible. "For the word of God is living and active. Sharper than any double-edged sword, it penetrates even dividing soul and spirit, joints and marrow; it judges the thoughts and attitudes of the heart" (Heb. 4:12).

Chapter 6

A Trip to Hell

"But the cowardly, the unbelieving, the vile, the murderers, the sexually immoral, those who practice magic arts, the idolaters and all liars—their place will be in the fiery lake of burning sulfur" (Rev. 21:8).

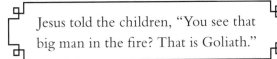

Jesus told the children, "You see that big man in the fire? That is Goliath."

On that same night the children saw Uncle Ken in heaven, Jesus taught them about the story of Elijah and the false gods. They read how Elijah had gone up into the mountains to prove to the people that he worshipped the one and only true God. After they finished with heaven, Jesus held the two boys by the hand, and they flew downwards very fast. They landed in hell!

Mungai said they heard people screaming and crying loudly in pain and saw fire everywhere. He related that the fire was so big, larger than our house. We live in a two-story maisonette.

Now picture a fire bigger than that! Then Jesus showed them a big, fat man who looked like a giant and was covered in fire. He was crying out for help. He must have been in great agony.

Jesus told the children, "You see that big man in the fire? That is Goliath."

Goliath is burning in hell! I thought to myself.

He lived centuries ago so that means he has been in hell for ages. That also means that each one of us will continue to live on after we die. Where will you live after you die? Will you live in heaven or hell? Mungai told me many people were burning in the fire and some ugly monsters were in hell. These could only be demons.

"Were you scared?" I asked him.

"No, Mum, we were not scared. Jesus made us bigger than the demons. The demons were scared of us. They were screaming and running away from us."

How awesome! This is in God's Word that we have power over the enemy. Jesus has given us authority to trample over Satan, the enemy. "I have given you authority to trample on snakes and scorpions and to overcome all the power of the enemy; nothing will harm you" (Luke 10:19).

Jesus told the boys that they had choice between heaven and hell. "Do you want Jesus and heaven, or do you want Satan and hell?"

He waited for them to answer. They quickly responded, "We want Jesus and heaven."

"Okay," he said.

He took them back to their homes and into their beds.

Ever since that day, I have been thinking about Goliath and how he has been burning in hell for centuries. How sad is this. He cannot and will never come out of hell. Hell is eternal damnation. As for those of us who are still alive, we have a chance to choose who to follow from this day onwards. We can choose who will be our master: Satan or God? You have only two options, and the choice is entirely yours. There is no in between. Despite their young age, Jesus asked the boys to make a choice. You also need to make this choice for yourself. You have heard the good news that Jesus Christ died on the cross and shed His blood so you and I can be forgiven for our sins. He rose from the dead on the third day, and He is alive. He is seated in heaven at the right hand of God the Father. Believe in Him today. Ask Him into your heart. Ask Him to forgive you of all your sins, and He will. Do not wait for another day because none of us knows when it will be our last day on this earth. Today is the day of salvation. "As has just been said: Today if you will hear His voice, do not harden your hearts as you did in the rebellion" (Heb. 3:15).

About Hell

Hell is believed to be downward; hence, it is most likely at the center of the earth, the core of the earth. It is a place where the wicked dead are punished for eternity. Other theories may indicate a different location of hell, but from the Scriptures, it is important to note that it is not a place for you or me. We need to know that it is a real place, and we should by all means avoid going there.

Jesus used this illustration to show how dreadful hell is.

If your hand causes you to sin, cut it off. It is better for you to enter life maimed than with two hands to go into hell where the fire never goes out. And if your foot causes you to sin, cut it off. It is better for you to enter life crippled than to have two feet and be thrown into hell. And if your eye causes you to sin, pluck it out. It is better for you to enter the kingdom of God with one eye than to have two eyes and be thrown into hell where 'their worm does not die, and the fire is not quenched (Mark 9:43–48).

Many verses in the Bible describe hell as a place of unquenchable fire; a place of torment, destruction, and wailing and gnashing of teeth; a place of fire and brimstone; a place of burning sulfur; a place of shame and contempt; and a bottomless pit or a lake of fire. It is sad to note that the torments in hell are never-ending.

Remember, Jesus showed the children Goliath burning in hell. This means he has been in hell for centuries and will be for many more to come. What a pity! Many people have a problem believing that a loving God can throw people into a place as bad as hell. There are those who believe that, once we get up there, God will forgive all of us and usher us into heaven. However, the truth is that God has a certain nature that cannot be changed. Whereas He is all loving and good, He is also holy, so He cannot tolerate any manner of sin. Sin separates us from God, but He is also merciful and freely pardons those who ask Him. Only those who have asked to be forgiven of their sins and have accepted Jesus Christ, the sacrificial Lamb of God, will escape hell.

Yes, hell is real, a place of indescribable torment and horror. It is a place where cries never cease and the fire is never quenched. It is important that we be aware of this place, no matter how disturbing or frightening it is. Nobody wants to hear that there is a place of damnation called hell where everything is hopeless forever and ever. Many people hope, albeit without much certainty, that heaven and hell do not exist and life ends right here on earth, but this is a deception from Satan. Satan is a deceiver and the father of all liars. The Bible commands us to resist him, and he will flee from us. However, if you don't resist him but choose to follow him, you will be cast out into hell, a place prepared for the devil and his angels.

"Then he will say to those on His left, 'Depart from me, you who are cursed, into the eternal fire prepared for the devil and his angels'" (Matt. 25:41). Those who end up in hell enter into eternal punishment, but the righteous enter into eternal life. No one who goes to hell deserved to go to heaven. Those in hell know that their punishment is just. They know exactly why they are in hell. They know they alone are to blame for being there.

> "And throw that worthless servant outside, into the darkness where there will be weeping and gnashing of teeth." *(*Matthew 25:30)

Hell is a place of fire that burns forever, and it burns the people who are in it. In the story of the rich man and Lazarus the beggar, the rich man calls out from hell and begs Lazarus to dip the tip of his finger in water and cool his tongue because he is in agony in the fire.

Several people have written about their encounters in hell. In *23 Minutes in Hell*, Bill Wiese talks of feeling incredibly thirsty while in hell and also talks about a filthy smell like that of burning sulfur. I believe this is the smell of burning flesh, which Revelation 14:10 describes. He also describes the darkness in hell, a darkness that fills one's heart with indescribable fear. Jesus picked Weise in the middle of night, just like the two boys, and dropped him into a cell in hell.

In *A Divine Revelation of Hell*, Mary K. Baxter writes about the terrible torments that she saw in hell. In the book, she provides a detailed description of people suffering and in great agony in this horrible place. Our Lord Jesus also showed her heaven and hell in a visit that lasted forty nights. At one point, the Lord allowed her to not only observe the goings on in hell but to also taste it so she could grasp the full meaning of the place.

Dr. Rawlings, a cardiologist, did a study of hell. His stories came from his heart patients who went to hell during resuscitation, came back to life, and told of the afterlife in hell. God gave these patients a second chance so they could tell us about this horrifying place. They, too, talk about an unquenchable fire, a choking smell, cries that never end, and an overwhelming fear. "And they will go out and look upon the dead bodies of those who rebelled against me; their worm will not die, nor will their fire be quenched, and they will be loathsome to all mankind" (Isa. 66: 24).

The suffering in hell is never-ending. The time to escape this fire is now. Once you die, it is too late. However, there is hope in Christ Jesus Our Lord. There is a place called heaven where those who believe in Him will go to after death. Heaven is a place full of bliss and happiness, a place where there is no more crying and no more pain. It is the exact opposite of hell. Hell was not made for you. It was prepared for Satan and his fallen angels after they rebelled against God.

God does not want you to go to hell, and that is why He gave Jesus, His one and only son, to die on the cross just for you. Through the blood that Jesus shed, you can be made clean, and you immediately become a child of God. This is your ticket to heaven!

Jesus Is in Our Everyday Life

On November 2, 2009, Mungai did not go to school, and Jesus visited him again. On this day, he felt a little under the weather, so I allowed him to stay home. I called him from work at about 10:00 a.m. to check on him.

He said, "Mum, Jesus is here in the room with me."

I was stunned and awed because that was the last thing I expected to hear from him. It was, however, reassuring to know that I would return home to find him well because the King of kings had come to watch over him. He had come to show him that He is our ever-present help in time of need. He had come to build confidence into my little boy's heart.

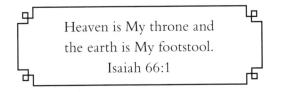

Heaven is My throne and
the earth is My footstool.
Isaiah 66:1

In the morning, as we were preparing to go downstairs for breakfast, I told Mungai to remember that he had asked God to help him not to cough during breakfast. Mungai had always coughed in the morning while eating. Mungai told me that he trusted God completely and I have to trust God completely as well. He sat on my bed and said something that has stuck with me ever since.

"God is so big. I saw Him seated in heaven, and His feet are here on earth."

How awesome and how true, I thought.

"Heaven is my throne and the earth is My footstool" (Isa. 66:1). Indeed, God is big, enormous, mighty, and all powerful. I thank God that Mungai stopped coughing during breakfast, which he now enjoys.

Jesus Talks to Mungai at 2 A.M.

On November 5, 2009, at exactly 2:00 a.m., Mungai sat up and nudged me to wake up.

I asked him, "What's wrong?"

He told me in a sleepy voice, "Jesus just spoke to me. He said, 'Mungai, I will come on Saturday to take you to heaven.'"

Jesus spoke to Mungai in the middle of the night at two in the morning. I stayed awake for a while longer. I was in wonder yet again. What was God teaching me? What was this incredible thing He had begun in my life? My son was visiting heaven, but it had a direct effect on me. I was the one being changed, being molded.

Jesus at a Birthday Party

The two boys share a birthdate so we have in the past years celebrated their birthdays together. They were both born on October 29 but a year apart. Mungai is the older one. We have been marveling at the fact that they share a birthday, they go to heaven together, and they both have a calling to serve Our Lord Jesus. That year, we had agreed to have their birthday on November 7, 2009, so Mungai's dad could attend because he was going to be away overseas on the actual birthdate. The party was to be an outdoor party by the pool because the boys wanted to swim. That whole week leading to the birthday, it had rained almost every day, but Jesus had promised Mungai that He would give him a good, fun-filled birthday without any rain and He would be present at the party.

The day before the party on Friday, it rained for the most part of the day. My friend Angie called me to say that the weather was not good for her children to swim. I told her not to worry. The Lord had said it would not rain on Saturday. She was a bit surprised by what I told her. Indeed, that Saturday, we woke up to a bright and beautiful sunny day. The birds were twitting, the sky was bright blue, and there was not a sign of rain. It was a perfect day for swimming, so we went to the Village Market and had a fantastic birthday party for Mungai and Mnjala. The day was so sunny and beautiful. Even the adults who usually shy away from taking a dip decided to swim, too. It was a total contrast from the previous day when it was rainy and cold for most of the day. We combined the boys' birthday party with the ones for my niece, Nzingo, and my nephew, Ryan. Nzingo is Pastor Chola's daughter, who, together with her little sister, Monje, were born after my brother's NDE.

At the end of the day, the two heaven boys confirmed that Jesus had been present at the party. He was in the swimming pool with them, and He was present at the time they were cutting their cakes, smiling at them. He never said anything to them, but He just smiled. Indeed, Jesus keeps His word. He never makes empty promises. "God is not a man that He should lie, nor a son of man that He should change His mind. Does He speak and then not act? Does He promise and not fulfill?" (Num. 23:19).

After the birthday, my friend Zenah came over to our house. As we were chatting, Mungai was seated on the living room floor playing with one of his new toys from his birthday presents.

After some time, Mungai, who was busy playing with his new toys, said, "Jesus is in the living room with us." He pointed to the area behind the television. "That is where Jesus is standing."

Zenah and I felt like blind bats. This being her first experience with this kind of thing, she begun to wonder what posture we should assume. "Should we bow down to worship, or what exactly should we do?"

I obviously had no response myself because I could not see Jesus either. After a couple minutes, Mungai told us that Angel Gabriel had come, and he was seated on the couch next to Zenah.

Zenah tried to pretend that she was touching the angel by stretching her left hand in the direction of the angel. Mungai said, "It is not possible to touch him, your hand is going past the angel." We had decided at this juncture to take the whole experience lightheartedly and just enjoy it.

We asked Mungai, "Do you feel scared when you see Jesus?"

"No, I feel love."

This is absolutely true according to the Bible. God is love.

Thereafter, we told him to ask Jesus a couple of question regarding Zenah's personal life. "Please ask Jesus when Zenah is going to get married?"

Mungai answered, "Jesus has said soon!"

Then Mungai said, "When I am in heaven, I do not feel like coming back home because heaven is so much fun! Mnjala and I have asked Jesus if we could remain in heaven but he told us that we have to return home." I guess it is not yet time for them to remain in heaven.

We asked him to describe Jesus.

"Jesus has holes on His hands and feet. I notice the holes every time I see Jesus. He wears shiny golden sandals on His feet."

Again, this is absolutely true. Jesus was crucified, and he bears the marks of crucifixion as a reminder of what He did for us His people, His precious creation. "Then He said to Thomas, 'Put your finger here; see my hands. Reach out your hand and put it into my side. Stop doubting and believe'" (John 20:27).

After a while, Mungai told Zenah that Jesus was seated in her car in the driver's seat. So we concluded that Jesus was going to take her home safely. This was good news for her. While coming over to our home that day, she had felt some kind of fear given the insecurity in Nairobi at night, but now all this fear had disappeared. She left a little after 9:00 p.m. and got home safely.

We quickly got ourselves ready for bed. Mungai was very tired because of all the swimming and playing. I thanked Our Lord Jesus for such a wonderful day. Later, I got on the phone with Zenah, and we chatted away, marveling at what the Lord was doing. Finally, when she hung up, I said a quick prayer and fell asleep. As I was dozing off, I sensed a heavy presence of God.

Chapter 7

God's Hands and Our Bodies

In the morning, Mungai woke up and immediately rushed to tell me, "Mum, I went to heaven."

I asked, "How did that happen?"

He giggled. "I just felt myself floating away upward through the roof. Angel Gabriel and Angel Michael were in the room. Jesus was here too, he was watching me to make sure that I am alright."

"I got to heaven, and Mnjala was there, too. We sat on the golden chair again. God started to teach us about the back again."

God told them that the back was a very important part of the body. He repeated what He had told them the first time. "Then he taught us about the eyes, elbow, knees, feet, and knuckles," Mungai said joyfully. "He said the eyes have three parts that work together to help us see. There is the white part, brown part, and black part inside. If the elbow is broken or injured, the hand will not be able to move. Also if the knee is injured, the whole leg will not be able to move. The foot helps you walk, and if it were not there, one would not be able to walk at all."

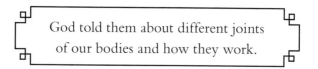

God told them about different joints of our bodies and how they work.

Mungai hopped around the living room, trying to show me how someone without a foot would behave. "See, if you do not have a foot, you cannot walk."

God then showed them His hands. "The fingers would not move if the knuckles are injured. One would not be able to move his or her fingers. They would remain still."

I was completely taken up by what my son was telling to me. It was incredible to hear him talking about the various parts of our bodies and how they function. And the fact he had learned this from the Creator Himself was dumbfounding. He could not have woken up with such a creative mind all of a sudden and made up such implausible stories with such insight. I believed with all my heart that the Lord was talking to him. The Lord has chosen him and his cousin for a purpose. God wants us to totally believe in him, and he is using little children to teach us who he is.

For weeks, I had been thinking about how God had shown the children His mighty hands. One Sunday afternoon, I was reading in the living room while Mungai was playing outside. After a short while, he came into the house.

"I want to tell you about God's hands," he said.

I was surprised. "Okay. What do you want to tell me?"

"I want to tell you that God's hands are very beautiful."

"What do you mean?"

"I can't explain it further. I just want you to know that God's hands are very beautiful. You remember that day when God showed Mnjala and me His hands?"

"Yes, I remember."

"God's hands are beautiful."

Sharing in Church

On this particular Sunday, I was scheduled to travel to Ethiopia that evening on a work assignment, so I did not have too much time to spend with Mungai. We planned to go for the praise and worship session at church and have lunch. It would leave me enough time to prepare for my trip. After the praise and worship session, the announcements were made. Then the children were called forward for prayer before departing for children's church. As soon as the prayers were done, Pastor George picked up Mungai and started asking him about heaven. I had previously never thought that we would have an opportunity to share some of the stories. I moved from my seat so I could stand next to Mungai. The pastor quickly gave me the microphone. What I shared must have come from the Holy Spirit. The next thing I saw was people in the congregation either gaping in complete amazement or crying. I talked about how Jesus Christ Our Lord had visited my son and nephew and how they had been shown heaven and hell.

My son did not understand why some people in the congregation were crying because heaven is a very good place anyway and God loves us all very much. Being an adult, I understood their tears to mean that Jesus had touched their hearts. Jesus wanted to do something in the hearts of His people. I fought so hard not to cry myself, as I shared this incredible story that Jesus had brought to our home. I knew He wanted it shared and He was using me as a vessel to do it.

Mungai's Dad and Jesus

It was November 12, 2009, and I was away in Axum again for work. As soon as I had settled down in my hotel room, I called home. I asked Mungai whether Jesus had visited, and he responded that he had and had seen Him twice. It appears odd for one to question her son about visiting heaven, but by this time, it had become a regular occurrence, part and parcel of our lives. The first time was the most significant, which I will relate in detail. The second time, Mungai was playing outside the house when he spotted a shining Jesus watching him.

The first time, as Mungai recounted to me, "Jesus was upstairs in your bedroom next to the curtains. He stood holding two swords in both hands."

He ordered Mungai in a loud voice, "Mungai, go tell your dad that I am here."

Mungai ran downstairs as fast as his little legs could carry him. He had to convey this message to his dad, who was in the dining area working on his laptop. Mungai let his dad know that Jesus was in our room upstairs carrying two swords. What he heard stunned Waiyaki. When I later queried him about what he felt about the incident, he responded that he was afraid to meet Jesus. So he just remained glued to his seat, wondering what to do, but did not go up to the room to confirm what Mungai had said.

To me, this was the best news I had heard in a long time. I definitely knew that God was at work. God was fighting for Mungai's daddy.

When we got married, we both loved and served the Lord, but my husband had drifted away from God over time. I had been praying for him for a long time, and I now had the assurance that God was doing something. It did not look like God had heard me because Waiyaki appeared impartial to the supernatural happenings in our home, but God had proven through this occurrence that He had not forgotten.

On this day, I was filled with joy and gratitude to my God. This was wonderful news! Dear reader, do not give up praying for your loved ones or the things you need. It may not appear like God is doing much sometimes because the signs are not evident but believe He is. He hears us when we pray. Though the answer tarries, hang in there. It will come. "For the revelation awaits an appointed time; it speaks of the end and will not prove false. Though it linger, wait for it; it will certainly come and will not delay" (Hab. 2:3).

God is fighting for Mungai's father because He does not want him to face the punishment reserved for those who have known the truth but turned away from it. It is imperative for those who have left the way of the Lord to get back on the right track.

The Bible in the book of Hebrews provides a description of the consequences of turning away from the knowledge of the truth. "If we deliberately keep on sinning after we have received the knowledge of the truth, no sacrifice for sins is left, but only a fearful expectation of judgment and of raging fire that will consume the enemies of God" (Heb. 10:26).

On this day, I was filled with joy and gratitude to my God. This was wonderful news!

Jesus Walks with Us

On November 27, 2009, I needed to go shopping, and my car would not start. As we sat in the car, Mungai told me that Jesus had come, gone under the car, and then quickly appeared inside the car in the backseat. Then he told me that the car would now start. And it did!

This was not the only time that the Lord intervened in my mechanical problems. Another opportunity came when my son and I had gone to our favorite Chinese restaurant near our home. When we finished lunch and were getting ready to go, alas, the car would not start. I began to think of who to call. I wondered whether I should call my husband or the automobile company that assists people when their cars have mechanical problems.

Mungai quickly told me, "Mum, please give me the car keys. Jesus has said that I start the car."

Without thinking, I gave my young son the car keys. I could not argue with him. I knew our Lord had asked him to ask for the keys.

Once he was in the driver's seat, he said, "Jesus has said that I start the car twice. The second time, it will start."

And it did! Praise the Lord!

Back to our story, we could now go shopping as planned. When we arrived at the shopping mall, Mungai mentioned that Angel Michael was there with us and he would stay with us until we finished shopping so nothing adverse happened to us. I went about shopping, thinking, pondering, and mulling over the words of my little boy.

I asked myself, *"You mean all the stories that we read in the Bible are true and that God indeed sent angels to watch over us?"* Yes, everything is true! The lesson here is that God is present in your life in the same way He is in mine and my son's life.

As we continued to do our shopping, Mungai said, "There are many toys in heaven in the toy room. Children in heaven are allowed to play as much as they want with the toys. The toys shine because they are made of gold."

"Some of the toys I have seen in heaven, I have never seen here on earth."

When we returned home, we found a gold-plated toy of an angel playing a harp in Mungai's box of toys. This toy had been there for a long time and he had even played with it, but he was now excited to find it because it reminded him of one of the toys in heaven.

"Aah Mum, it looks like one of the toys I have played with in heaven, only that the one in heaven shined so much more."

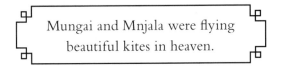

Mungai and Mnjala were flying beautiful kites in heaven.

That evening, Mungai told me that he wished that he could fly a kite. I told him to ask Jesus to grant him his request. That night, he went to heaven, and he flew a shiny red kite while his cousin Mnjala flew a shiny blue one. He reported they had had so much fun with very beautiful kites pulling them upwards. Don't forget that these two children were taken to heaven from their separate homes and were only reporting their escapades the next morning.

I called my sister Janet and talked to my little nephew Mnjala, who confirmed that what my son was saying matched his story. I was awed!

On Sunday, November 29, 2009, my sister Janet came home with her children so we could go to church together. While we were seated in church, Mungai and Mnjala said they could see Angel Gabriel near the altar. After the church service, they reported to us that this angel was with them until Sunday school ended. As we drove to the airport to pick up another sister of mine and her husband, the children said Jesus was in the car with us. I have really been enjoying these mighty visitations from God. They have built up my faith in leaps and bounds. I have since grown in the Lord. Everything about me has changed: my dreams, plans, perspective toward life, motives, attitudes, values, and relationships with family, friends, and society as a whole. I enjoy talking about Jesus because I would want everyone to know Him. I want as many as possible to believe in Jesus.

The following week, as Mungai and I were on our way to a shopping mall, we were held up in some traffic. Mungai told me that Jesus was standing outside by an advertising pole looking at us and what was going on around. Afterwards, as we were getting back home, Mungai mentioned that Jesus was in the car with us. I started to praise God and worship His holy name. I was trying to get accustomed to these stories, but I realized I will never get used to them. God is so good! God is great! May He receive glory and honor through this book.

Chapter 8

Sharing the Good News with Others

One evening, I went to pick up Mungai's friend Kibet and his sister Chelangat, who were coming to our house for a sleepover. As the children were happily playing and sharing stories, Chelangat asked me to call her mother to come and pick her up. She had changed her mind about staying over for the night. I guessed she was too young at the time for a sleepover. Their mother Angie came to pick her up, accompanied by her brother Kim. Angie had previously expressed concern about her brother not believing in God. Mungai had been to their house a few days earlier and narrated to Kim about how he had been seeing Jesus so Kim decided to come over because he wanted to know more about this. This was an opportune moment to tell him about the existence of God. We had a long conversation, and I was glad he listened because he seemed to be having a change of heart.

When they were about to leave, Kim asked Mungai, "When will Jesus visit you next?"

Mungai said, "Jesus has told me that He will visit me tonight."

I was surprised at how bold and confident my son had become. He had learned to totally trust in God and know that, when Jesus promises to visit, He does. This has also rubbed off on me. I trust in Jesus with everything I have got. He is real, and He is a good God.

The following day, we spent the morning chatting with my husband Waiyaki, and I forgot to ask Mungai whether Jesus had visited, although I remembered sensing the presence of God that night.

I heard myself whispering, "Jesus is here."

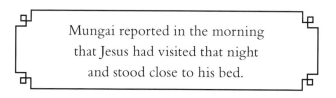

Mungai reported in the morning that Jesus had visited that night and stood close to his bed.

When I got to work, I called home and spoke to Mungai. He confirmed that Jesus had indeed visited that night and stood close to his bed.

Sharing with Relatives

We had a cousin's wedding to attend on December 12, 2009, so we proceeded to my parents' home. This was where my cousin Kezia was to be picked from, as per our culture, which requires that the groom's family pick up the bride from her home on her wedding day. Both Mungai and Mnjala were the designated page boys.

When we got to my parents' house, I found relatives had gathered from our up-country regions of Mombasa and Taita, and guests filled the house. I got an opportunity to share with my uncles about the visitations my son and my nephew had been having. It was awesome! There was a move of God, and I could see that my uncles were visibly touched. They had tears in their eyes as I shared these wonderful experiences with them.

My Aunty Hilary, who has an equally incredible story to tell, joined in the conversation. She also had a trip to heaven. Many years ago, she had become sick and died for a couple hours. Jesus showed her heaven. With tears in her eyes, she testified that heaven is indeed a real place. I thank God that she can back up the boys' stories of heaven.

She told her brothers, "Believe that these children have seen heaven. It is real."

Aunty Hilary's Story

Aunty Hilary's story is amazing because, when she fell sick in May 1980, the doctors were unable to diagnose the disease. They carried out all the tests that could possibly be done, but they could not detect any disease in the results. She was, however, critically ill and had to be admitted to a hospital. The doctors resolved to put her on painkillers and a drip because she was suffering from excruciating pain. Her whole body, right through into the bone marrow, was aching, and she was unable to eat or drink anything. Her condition deteriorated, and one early morning in the second week, she died. While her family members were mourning her here on earth, her spirit was in heaven. She does not know how she got to heaven. She remembers entering through a very large and beautiful pearly gate shaped like an arch. Right inside this gate was a beautiful angel, smartly dressed with a large book resembling a very large Bible. She asked the angel whether that was a Bible, but the angel did not respond. She walked to the left side of the table, where she had a better view of the book. She noticed very many names were written in that big book. The angel was patiently looking for her name, turning page after page, but her name could not be found. Her name was missing from the book! This was the Lamb's book of life written about in the book of Revelation. "Nothing impure will ever enter it, nor will anyone who does what is shameful or deceitful, but only those whose names are written in the Lamb's book of life" (Rev. 21:27).

Immediately, a beautiful little girl with long hair came and held Aunty Hilary's hand. She escorted her to another place where they passed through another arch-shaped gate. Inside this gate was a great multitude of people. These people were very many, stretching as far as her eyes could see. They were all dressed in white robes, and their faces and robes were shining brightly. They were beaming with joy and filled with peace and tranquility. More interestingly, they were singing beautiful songs to God. They sang new songs that my aunty had never heard here on earth. To date, she cannot remember any of those songs. She yearned to be a part of this massive choir and wanted to join in the singing, but when she tried to join them, she realized she could not reach them. A big ridge was between the heavenly choir and herself. She lifted her foot as if to try to cross over, but she quickly realized that she would fall into what looked like a pit, leading to a dark, horrid place beneath her.

While all this was going on in heaven, here on earth, her people were mourning over the death of Aunty Hilary. Phone calls were being made around the country to let relatives and friends know about her demise. We were in Nairobi at the time, and I can vividly remember our phone ringing and a sad Uncle Wilson informing us that our aunty was no more.

God has a sense of humor sometimes. My uncles could not come to an agreement as to which mortuary to take her body, so it lay covered in one of the hospital rooms waiting for the decision to be made. However, this turned out to be a blessing in disguise because God had planned that Aunty Hilary would return to planet Earth, to her body that was waiting safely in the hospital.

Back in heaven, Aunty Hilary finally resolved in her heart to praise God from where she was. Her heart was full of joy as she worshipped with the souls in heaven. She wanted to be in heaven because she could see the glory of God from where the worshippers were. The light from God shone all over, and it was a beautiful sight to behold. Heaven glittered, as it had streets of gold. After a while, one of the worshippers in heaven waved his right hand at her as if to send her away. Immediately after this, she found herself back in her body and in the hospital bed.

One of her brothers, Uncle Wilson, was sitting next to her covered body crying when he noticed some movement. He called out to her, "Hilary, are you okay?"

She responded, "Yes, I am okay."

"Do you know who I am?"

"You are my brother Wilson."

At this time, she could hear and talk, but she could not see. She had become blind.

It was total pandemonium at the hospital when everyone got to hear that Aunty Hilary was alive again. The doctor who had declared her dead was called back to see the miracle. My Uncle Wilson is also a medical doctor, and he, too, had certified that she had died. He was baffled but happy to see his sister alive again. The nurses were in awe. The doctor put her back on a drip as she was very weak and still in pain. She says she was in perfect health while in heaven.

Later that night, God blew air into her eyes, and she received her sight. Then she heard the voice of God telling her, "Deuteronomy 32:39. See now that I myself am He! There is no God besides me. I put to death, and I bring to life. I have wounded, and I will heal. And no one can deliver out of my hand."

A few days later, she asked the doctor to discharge her. Though she was still very weak, the doctor bowed down to her persistent plea to leave the hospital. She had a small baby at home and wanted to see him.

While at home, some two friends came to visit her. During their visit, they shared the good news of salvation with Aunty Hilary and led her to the Lord. As soon as she accepted Jesus as her Lord and Savior, God's hand came down and lifted her from the seat. She says she felt as though a huge tractor had come and scooped her out of the sofa. She immediately found herself standing, something she had not been able to do since leaving hospital. At that moment, God lifted her hands up, and she was able to worship Him. Then very quickly, God placed her into a kneeling position, and she continued to worship Him. For almost four hours, my aunty and her two friends worshipped. When they finally stopped, Aunty Hilary was completely healed. Praise God! I thank God for the two women who came to my aunty and shared the good news with her.

Thank God that He was so gracious to her. Thank God that He allowed her to return to her body and gave her another opportunity to get things right with Him. She told me that she will forever be grateful for that second chance that God gave her because, if not, she would have been in hell burning because her name was not in the Lamb's book of life. For over thirty years now, she would be in the dark burning pit suffering and still counting because eternity has no end.

However, do not rely on this one experience thinking that God will definitely give you a second chance. You need to make a decision right away concerning where you will go after you die. The decision is entirely ours. You now know the way to heaven. It is through Jesus Christ, God's son.

In 1984, Aunty Hilary died again briefly. A doctor who was unaware of her allergy to penicillin gave her an injection of the medicine. This time round, she found herself going up a ladder that was going straight up to heaven. The ladder was brilliant white in color. She was climbing on the right side, and people were moving downwards on the left side of the ladder. As I listened to Aunty Hilary's story, I was reminded of Genesis 28:10.

> Jacob left Beersheba and set out for Haran. When he reached a certain place, he stopped for the night because the sun had set. Taking one of the stones there, he put it under his head and lay down to sleep. He had a dream in which he saw a stairway resting on the earth, with its top reaching to heaven and the angels of God were ascending and descending on it.

How amazing is this? Aunty Hilary saw the ladder that Jacob of the Old Testament saw. This is proof yet again that heaven has always been in existence.

Aunty Hilary returned to her bed and found one of the patients had been praying for her to get better. God had answered the prayer, and now Aunty Hilary has lived to tell us that heaven is real. Wherever and whenever she gets the opportunity, she talks about her experience so the lost may find Christ.

Indeed, Jesus commanded that the Good News be shared around the world. It is important that as many people as possible are saved so they can have eternal life in heaven with God. It is mandatory that we Christians tell others about God so more people hear the Good News and come to the knowledge of Christ. The gospel of Jesus Christ has to go far and wide. We all need to take a part in this. Our reward is in heaven. The more we reach out to others, the bigger the reward. Life is about God. Others can only find the love God has for us through another being. Use whatever gift that God has put in you to reach out to others.

"He said to them, 'Go into all the world and preach the good news to all creation. Whoever believes and is baptized will be saved but whoever does not believe will be condemned'" (Mark 16:15).

Another Teaching from the Throne Room

My cousin's wedding was very beautiful and colorful, and we spent the whole day there. Afterwards, we left with my mother and my sister Janet and dropped them off at my mum's house. By this time, it had become dark and was threatening to rain, so I said a short prayer for protection. The children told me that Jesus was in the car with us so I did not have to worry.

As my mum was coming out of the car, Mungai told her that her house was blessed because he could see two angels in her house. One angel was upstairs; another was downstairs. This made my mother immediately burst out into praise and rejoicing to the Lord.

We set off for home together with Mnjala, as he was coming over to our house for a sleepover. When we reached one of the many roundabouts on the highway, I was unable to cross over to the other side because the traffic lights were not working. As is custom in our country, it is rare for motorists to give each other way. By this time, the rain was pouring hard, and my vision became blurred. Combined with the fact that the cars were coming really fast with full headlights, I really was stuck! I said a small prayer asking God to send a traffic policeman to stop the cars. Immediately, a policeman who was standing uninterestedly together with others under an umbrella jumped onto the road and stopped the oncoming cars and asked me to go.

He said, "*Mama enda!*"[2]

Amen! This was yet another answered prayer.

---

2   In the Kiswahili language, this means, "Mother or Woman, you go!"

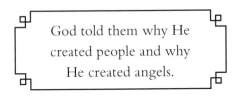

God told them why He
created people and why
He created angels.

When we got home, the boys had dinner, showered, and got ready for bed. They were so excited to be together, laughing and sharing different toys. They told me that they felt in their hearts that they would go to heaven again that night. They amazed me when they said this. I realized they were beginning to sense God in their hearts. They could hear Jesus' voice in their hearts. I asked them to hop into their bed and choose a story from the Children's Bible. They chose the story of Paul, and I read it to them and said a prayer. And we were off to bed.

In the morning, the children told me that they were in heaven.

My son said, "Mum, I was flying a shiny red kite, and Mnjala had a shiny blue kite. It was so much fun because the kites were lifting us up. There were other children and people playing with us, too."

I was very pleased to know that we are going to play in heaven. A little child in all of us wants to play. These heavenly kites seem like one of a kind. They actually fly with you. I cannot imagine how much fun this must be!

God called out in a loud voice, "Mungai and Mnjala, come here!"

Mungai told God that they were returning their kites to the toy room. As soon as they were done, they found themselves in the throne room in front of God, seated on the golden chair.

God told them that He was going to tell them why He created people and why He created angels. "I created people so they can praise and worship me."

Then He taught the boys why he created the heavenly beings. "I created angels so some of the angels can be in heaven to worship me. I sent others to earth to fight Satan and his demons so they do not disturb my people. Then I sent other angels to earth to heal my people."

What an incredible truth! God made us so we can worship Him. That was His sole reason for making man. He created man in His image. "So God created man in His own image, in the image of God He created him; male and female He created them" (Gen. 1:27).

The boys' account of why God created the angels is also in line with the Holy Scriptures. The two verses below are about the worshipping angels; the next one talks of the ministering angels. God sent these angels to heal, strengthen, encourage, and rescue His people.

- "Praise Him, all His angels, praise Him all His heavenly hosts" (Ps. 148:2).
- "All the angels were standing around the throne and around the elders and the four living creatures. They fell down on their faces before the throne and worshipped God, saying: Amen! Praise and glory and wisdom and thanks and honor and power and strength be to our God forever and ever. Amen" (Rev. 7:11).
- "An angel from heaven appeared to Him and strengthened Him" (Luke 22:43).

Mungai and Mnjala Share in Church

We attended the Sunday service as usual at Eagle's Faith Christian Centre on the morning of December 13, 2009. Before departing for children's church, Pastor George asked Mungai and Mnjala to tell the church about heaven.

He asked them, "When have you last visited heaven?"

To everyone's shock and surprise, they replied, "Yesterday at night."

There was a sober mood in the congregation as Mungai shared this incredible visitation to heaven and how Our Mighty God had spoken to them from His mighty white throne. He explained what God taught them about people and angels. I also shared some of the stories Mungai had told me on previous days. I elaborated a little regarding what I felt in my heart about everything that God was trying to teach through these children.

At the end of this wonderful session, the pastor asked Mungai to pray for the church. I wondered what he was going to say, but I remembered it was not my business but God's. He proceeded to pray, and the Lord obviously gave him the words. He asked Jesus to bless everyone who had come to church that day. He prayed that God would help them be good and kind to each other, and he prayed for God to visit them as well. Then the pastor took the microphone and continued in prayer.

After church, we went to buy lunch. As we were driving home, the children told me that Jesus was in the car with us. I quickly said, "Ask Him whether He was glorified in church when we shared."

They responded, "He can hear you, and He has answered in a very big voice yes!"

I cannot express what I felt. I praised God with all my heart.

God Tells the Boys about Planet Earth

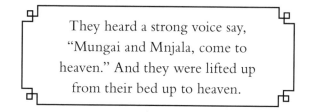

They heard a strong voice say, "Mungai and Mnjala, come to heaven." And they were lifted up from their bed up to heaven.

On that Thursday, December 17, 2009, we headed off to a shopping mall with the two boys. Curious to find out whether they had been to heaven again, I posed this question to them, "Boys, did you guys go to heaven last night?"

They answered in unison, "Yes." Mnjala proceeded to say, "God called out to us with a very strong voice, he said, 'Mungai and Mnjala, come to heaven!'"

Immediately, they were lifted up from their bed. They were laughing as they described how they had been half asleep until they started to see the planets. Then they went higher and higher upwards and entered heaven through a window. They went upstairs, where God was seated on His throne.

"Mum, heaven shines so much. It is made out of gold," Mungai said delightfully.

They said they sat on a golden chair that divided itself and became two golden chairs. Then God went on to teach them about the earth and the planets.

He said to them, "I made the earth so my people can live there happily, and I made the planets so my people can look at the planets and know I am God."

Then God told the children something I found very interesting. "Mungai and Mnjala, I will make you scientists." God also added something to this which I will not reveal at this time. God is God, and He can do anything and everything. We will wait to see Him fulfill His promises.

That evening before we went to bed, I told the boys that, when they visited heaven again, they should ask God for what they need. Mnjala needed to ask that his nose stop running all the time; Mungai needed to ask for his dad to feel better. I was telling them this as I sat on the first step of the stairway. They pointed behind me, saying that Jesus was right there behind me. This overwhelmed me so much that I began to pray and praise Him. What an honor and privilege for me to encounter God in such a way.

Chapter 9

God Loves All the People of the Earth

On the following day, December 18, 2009, Mungai and Mnjala informed me that they had visited heaven during the night. I was very curious to find out how they got to heaven. They told me that Jesus, who was watching them from heaven this time, gave them wings, with which they flew upwards to heaven. Jesus just watched them from heaven to make sure they got there safely.

As they approached heaven, Jesus told them, "Enter heaven through the window."

When they arrived, they sat on the golden chair again in front of God Almighty.

> God told them, "The most important planet to me is planet Earth because that is where all the people I created live, and I love them very much."

They said it was as though God had opened a small window. Below which, they could see all the planets from heaven.

God told them, "The most important planet to me is planet Earth because that is where all the people I created live, and I love them very much, each one of them. I created the other planets so that, when my people on earth see these planets, they will know I am real."

Then the children made their prayer requests, the ones we had discussed before they went to bed the previous night. Mnjala asked God to stop his runny nose, cough, and rashes that were bothering him.

And God said, "Okay."

Mungai thereafter asked for healing for his daddy.

God answered, "He shall be well." The boys resonated this together.

Then the boys recounted how they returned home in very beautiful multicolored parachutes. Jesus had given them instructions regarding how to use them. He told them that they needed to pull on the left side, so once they got to the planets, they pulled onto something on the left. They added that they saw all the planets once again and they followed all the instructions the Lord had given them. The parachutes got them up to the front of the window of their bedroom.

Mungai said that they got in through the window "like angels." "Our fingers passed through and then our hands and bodies."

"We were in our spirits!" Mungai cheerfully narrated.

I wondered where he had learned this word "spirit" from.

"How did you know the word spirit?"

"I just knew in my heart that we were in our spirits."

"Our bodies were on the bed and we entered back into our bodies and covered ourselves."

Mnjala added that, once they were in bed, Jesus whispered in their hearts. He told them, "Good night."

About the Planets

When God told the children about the planets, I became curious to know what was so amazing about them to warrant the fact that they contribute to the revelation of the existence of God.

Indeed, as I started to study them, I was very fascinated by how incredible God's creation is. Everything he created is breathtaking, unfathomable, beautiful, splendid, majestic, and incredibly awesome. Scientists have written books upon books about the universe, and they are still discovering new things. They know from what they have discovered that there is still so much more yet to be uncovered and that what they know is just a drop in the ocean. Scientists do not even have telescopes big enough to capture all the galaxies because of the vastness of the same.

The word of God says that the heavens tell of the glory of God. The skies declare His might. "The heavens declare the glory of God; the skies proclaim the work of His hands" (Ps. 19:1).

According to science, the world came to being through a big bang, and then the creation of the universe was set into motion. I always ask myself, "What caused the big bang?" The truth is, big bang or not, God created the heavens and the earth, as the Bible has revealed to us. He made all things. He said, "Let there be," and there was. "In the beginning God created the heavens and the earth" (Gen. 1:1).

God created hundreds of billions of galaxies. The one where planet Earth is seated on is called the Milky Way, and it contains over 200 billion stars. Imagine just one star can be the size of planet Earth. Now picture billions of those hanging out there just in our galaxy! The Milky Way is in the shape of a spiral that is 100,000 light-years in diameter. A light-year is a unit of length equal to just under 10 trillion kilometers, as the International Astronomical Union defines. Can you picture how vast this galaxy is? We cannot describe this! Our minds cannot even begin to picture the vastness of the universe.

The sun is the largest star, and it is a colossal raging ball of fire. The temperatures are about 10,000 degrees Fahrenheit. We are 93 million miles away from the sun, but we still feel its heat and see its light. The sun is 1.3 million times larger than planet Earth is. The sun's diameter is 1,392,000 kilometers while the Earth's is 12,756 kilometers. Can you fathom that? The Earth is basically a tiny ball compared to the sun. As we know, the Earth is very large with seven continents that are each incredibly vast. If you have ever travelled by plane, you are able to look down and see how large the surface of the Earth is. The sun is way larger than this by over a million times!

Of the eight planets, Jupiter is the largest of them all. It's over 317 times larger than planet Earth is. It is pretty amazing that God in His might made such incredible bodies that hang out in space held by nothing else but gravity. The whole universe is so massive to the extent that our minds cannot even begin to comprehend. The scientists cannot have a telescope big enough to see and take pictures of the unknown universe. This is how great and mighty God is. "Praise Him, you highest heavens and you waters above the skies. Let them praise the name of the Lord, for He commanded and they were created" (Ps. 148:5).

Yes, God in His might and power created everything. He created all the heavenly bodies. He said, "Let there be!" and there was.

A Guardian Angel

We had gone out for a day of swimming on December 23, 2009, together with my sister Esther and her husband Sascha, who were on holiday in Kenya from Germany. Our other siblings, together with their children, had also come to spend the day at the Village Market, an enjoyable recreation center in the outskirts of Nairobi. My dad was also present in the group.

We stopped swimming sometime before four o'clock and relocated to a nearby fast-food restaurant to have something to bite. Just before we left, to our surprise, it started raining cats and dogs. A huge traffic jam built up in the whole city. Much later in the evening news, we found out that the rain had caused a lot of havoc and destruction around the city. Trees and billboards had fallen on cars, and at least four people had lost their lives.

Before we got to see the news, however, we were stuck in the traffic jam for quite a while. My dad and Sascha decided to use a different route to get to my place while Esther, Mungai, and I took another. As we were sitting in the car wondering what was causing such traffic, a man dressed in a brand-new security guard uniform suddenly appeared and came to my window. I was surprised at myself because I did not feel afraid of him as he knocked persistently at my window. His new uniform and kind-looking face encouraged me to slide down my window to hear what he had to say.

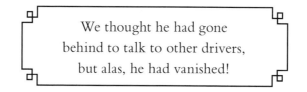

We thought he had gone behind to talk to other drivers, but alas, he had vanished!

He explained to us that an enormous tree had just fallen a few meters ahead of us and this was causing the traffic buildup. We were glad that we finally knew what was happening ahead. What was interesting about this encounter was that this guard suddenly disappeared. We did not see him again. We thought he had gone behind to talk to other drivers, but alas, he had vanished! We tried to look back to see whether he was among the few people who were bravely walking in the rain, but we could not see him. Later on, as Esther and I were recounting this incidence, we said that we both thought that this man had been an angel. He must have been. We could find no other explanation.

As I have come to learn, God is in the business of protecting His people. He sends His angels to encamp around those who love Him. He makes sure of their safety.

> If you make the Most High your dwelling—even the Lord, who is my refuge—then no harm will befall you, no disaster will come near your tent. For He will command His angels concerning you to guard you in all your ways, they will lift you up in their hands, so that you will not strike your foot against a stone (Ps. 91:9–12).

Christmas with Jesus

I was looking forward to Christmas Day, as Jesus had promised Mungai that he would spend the day with us. Mungai, his dad, and I had a wonderful time shopping and buying presents for different family members prior to this day. We recounted how God had been so faithful to us and provided for us. God had blessed us, so we wanted to bless others, too. We always spend Christmas Day together with my in-laws and their children at my parents-in-laws' home within Nairobi.

On Christmas Day, just as he had promised, Jesus visited us. He appeared to Mungai early in the morning as soon as he woke up. On our way to my parents-in-laws' house in Karen, Mungai saw Jesus in the car. While at Karen, Mungai saw Him outside where the barbecue meat was being prepared for our big Christmas feast. Jesus towered over Mungai's grandfather, dad, and uncles as they roasted the meat over a big grill in the back yard. To crown it all, Jesus was there when we all gathered for the final meeting and prayers before we left for our various homes.

I felt in my heart to share with the family members about Mungai's experiences.

Then Mungai pointed to the middle of the living room. "Jesus is here. He is standing right there."

We all became silent. I realized then that I was still not accustomed to all these supernatural encounters. I finally suggested that we talk to Jesus because He was present with us. Mungai told the children that nobody should laugh when we talk to Jesus. I asked Mungai to share one story about heaven and God. He told them about what God said about him being a scientist if he remained obedient. Ryan narrated a little about what happened when Mungai spent a night at their house. It was the day when God allowed Mungai to see their late Uncle Ken in heaven.

Ryan added that Mungai was so blessed and he would become very famous for God. Mungai said that Jesus told him that Ryan would also see Jesus when he is a little older. My sister-in-law Annie was the first one to talk to Jesus. She asked Him to heal her. Mungai told her that Jesus had responded that she would be healed soon. Then she asked about her mother who had been ailing for some time. She said she wanted to know when her mother would get well.

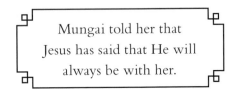

Mungai told her that
Jesus has said that He will
always be with her.

Mungai responded that Jesus said He would not say when she would be healed, but He wanted her to know that, when she goes to visit her mum at home one day, she would find that she had been healed. I wondered what this meant.

My niece, who was in high school, spoke next. She told Jesus that she had so many subjects in school that she felt overwhelmed and confused. Mungai told her that Jesus responded that He would always be with her. Hearing this, she broke down and cried. We were filled with awe and wonder, and our eyes welled up with tears.

My mother-in-law also asked for her healing. Mungai told her that Jesus was right there and He was listening to her. At that point, Ryan thanked Jesus for visiting us, and he told Jesus that this was our best Christmas ever because He had visited us. I imagined that Jesus was with millions of other Christians who were celebrating His birthday around the world.

Mungai informed us that Jesus said He would be with us until everyone departed to his or her homes. At this juncture, everyone started thanking Mungai.

Mungai quickly said, "Do not thank me. Thank Jesus. He is here. It is not me. It is Jesus."

So we all felt rebuked and said "Thank you!" to the right person, Jesus Christ, the Son of the Living God.

Christmas has always been a special time for me, but this one was the best one ever!

Chapter 10

Jesus Continues to Visit Mungai and Mnjala

On December 28, 2009, I was just about to start reading a Bible story for Mungai before his bedtime.

He exclaimed, "Jesus has appeared, and he is standing in front of the television. He said, 'Mungai, you shall come to heaven tonight.'"

I sat there for a moment wondering silently. Then I cleared my throat and proceeded to read the story.

The following day, Mungai told me that he was in heaven with his cousin Mnjala and they had played a lot.

"It was so much fun!" He continued to narrate how they were swimming and that, when they were in heaven, they were able to swim and breathe underwater. He told me beautiful fish with many colors were in this water and the fish were not scared of them.

"We can touch the fish under the water," Mungai tried to explain to me as I gazed at him puzzled but excited.

He described the swimming suits they wore in heaven as being gold in color. He was equally excited when he told me there were many water slides in heaven and they had played there, too.

"Mum, it was so much fun!"

I believed him.

On January 5, 2010, while in the car on our way to the supermarket, I asked Mungai whether he missed going to heaven. It had been over a week since his last visit.

He paused and said, "Jesus had whispered, 'Mungai, do not miss going to heaven. I shall take you to heaven today.'"

I thought to myself that it really did not matter when he was taken to heaven or whether he was taken at all. God was in control of what happened to him.

The following day, I had yet another story to record in this book. It sounded just like what happened the last time the two boys had been to heaven. Mungai said his cousin was there, too. They were in the water swimming again, and they knew how to swim. Mungai said everybody in heaven knew how to swim. Here on earth, Mungai did not know how to swim. He enjoyed being in water that was not above his head. He would rather have floaters around his waist or arms. It is mind-boggling that he is not only able to swim in heaven but also breathe underwater.

Jesus in Mombasa

On January 14, 2010, Mungai and I were in an airplane on our way to Mombasa, a coastal town in the southern part of Kenya. A cousin of mine was getting married that weekend, so we felt that it would be an ideal time to have a short holiday, thus killing two birds with one stone. We would enjoy the beach and attend the wedding. As soon as we boarded the aircraft, I said a short prayer to ask for God's protection. Mungai and I sat on the right side of the plane about two or three seats behind the right wing.

Mungai quickly mentioned to me that Angel Gabriel was seated at the wing of the airplane. I was tongue-tied.

"What? Angel Gabriel is seated at the wing of the aircraft?" I had tears in my tears.

"Mum, why are you crying?"

I really didn't know what to respond to my boy.

"God sent Angel Gabriel to make sure we got to Mombasa safely. He will be with us until we land."

God indeed sends His angels to guard His people.

> "If you make the Most High your dwelling- even the Lord, who is my refuge- then no harm will befall you, no disaster will come near your tent. For he will command His angels concerning you to guard you in all your ways; they will lift you up in their hands, so that you will not strike your foot against a stone" (Ps. 91:9–12).

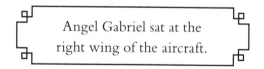

Angel Gabriel sat at the right wing of the aircraft.

When we landed, Mungai's ears were blocked. They had been blocked since we began the descent to Mombasa. I advised him to chew some gum, but this did not help. Next I asked him to swallow his saliva to try to unblock his ears, but this did not help either. Finally, we disembarked and boarded a taxi. While in the taxi, Mungai said that Jesus told him to open his mouth. When he did, his ears popped open.

"Mum, you know who is in control of everything?"

I smiled as I thought to myself, *I should be the one telling you this!*

That evening, we went out for dinner at the *Tamarind Dhow* together with my sister Monje and her husband Kamau. While we were in the dhow waiting for it to sail into the ocean, Mungai pointed at the sail and said Angel Michael was seated there. We all looked in wonder because we could not see a thing. We, however, marveled at how God was protecting us and knew we would have a safe and fun ride.

As soon as the dhow started moving, Mungai said Angel Michael had exchanged with Jesus. Jesus was now the one at the sail. That was it for us. We stopped everything and began to pray and praise our Lord and Savior. We talked about the many stories in the Bible that revolve around Jesus being in water. I felt as though I had been transported to the days when Jesus lived, preached, and healed on earth. Many times, Jesus preached from a boat. I remembered the stories about how He walked on water and how He calmed a storm while at sea with His disciples and many others. Now here we were at sea, in an old dhow accompanied by Jesus. The feeling of gratitude that I felt cannot be expressed.

Mungai said that he felt in his heart that Jesus would stay with us until we went back to the hotel. He, however, did not have a chance to tell us the end of the story because Mungai was fast asleep by the time the dhow docked back to the hotel. The day had been too exciting, between our arrival at the beautiful *Papweza Hotel*, to all the swimming and time on the beach, and finally dinner on the dhow. My little boy was tired out.

The following day, we spent the whole afternoon at the beach again, swimming and having a marvelous time. While we were in the water, Mungai told us that Angel Gabriel, Angel Michael, and Jesus were present with us. He said that Jesus had split Himself into three. Two of Him was there with us. The other one was near a boat that was a bit far off in the horizon. As usual like blind bats, we kept looking, wondering, and listening. Mungai said he was touching Angel Gabriel with his toes and that Angel Gabriel had told him it was okay. It was about time I learned how to take all this in because God had chosen this for my son. My sister Monje and I made a few jokes, telling Mungai not to go into the deep waters so the angels did not panic in a bid to save him. We had a wonderful afternoon.

The wedding was very enjoyable. We had a wonderful time and got to see many relatives we had not seen in a long time. My Aunty Hillary was among the guests at the wedding. She again wanted to hear the stories about the two boys visiting heaven at the same time. She was particularly interested because, as I narrated earlier, she also had an encounter with God. She had died and gone to heaven. The doctor had certified her death, and then like magic, she returned from the dead with this unbelievable story about heaven. She has lived for God ever since that day.

Dear reader, heaven and hell are real. They are not a figment of somebody's imagination.

> The names of those who have accepted Jesus Christ into their hearts, who have been born again, are written in the Lamb's book of life.

Let me repeat that, when Aunty Hillary was in the presence of God in heaven, she was not born again. An angel at heaven's gates was looking for her name in a book, but it was missing. She was just about to be cast into the darkness, but God had mercy on her. She returned to her lifeless body in the hospital. Everyone in the hospital was amazed, including the doctor who had confirmed her death. She had come back to life! "Nothing impure will ever enter it, nor will anyone who does what is shameful or deceitful, but only those whose names are written in the Lamb's book of life" (Rev. 22:7).

Undeniably, the names of those who have accepted Jesus Christ into their hearts, who have been born again, are written in the Lamb's book of life. Ensure that yours is in that book today. Ask Jesus into your heart, and He will come in and change your life. It does not matter what you did in the past. God forgives and forgets. As far as the east is from the west, so far will God take away all your sins. Nobody is perfect. God's Word puts it plainly. Just accept Jesus. It is a simple message. "For all have sinned and fall short of the glory of God" (Rom. 3:23). "For the wages of sin is death, but the gift of God is eternal life in Christ Jesus our Lord" (Rom. 6:23).

Our Return Journey from Mombasa

On our return journey to Nairobi, we were again seated three seats behind the right wing. It is interesting because I never asked for those particular seats. God must have prearranged it. This time, Mungai said Angel Michael was at the wing of the aircraft. I asked him to describe the angel. I noticed he was looking out of the window intently as he tried to describe him. He was definitely seeing something I was not!

He looked out downward through the plane's window, like he was stretching to see something outside. Then he whispered into my ear, "He is wearing brown sandals. They are brown, but they are shining. He is also wearing something that looks like a white dress with a gold belt at the waist. He is shining. Even his eyes are shining, and he is looking at us. The angel is going to stay there until we land in Nairobi."

"How do you know that?"

"In my heart."

When we landed in Nairobi, he said, "Angel Michael is standing at the wing." When the aircraft came to a stop, he said, "The angel has disappeared."

Yes, God always sends angels to protect His people. I have proved this now more than once.

The Music Room in Heaven

> Mungai said to me that Jesus had just spoken to him. He said, "Mungai, you shall visit heaven again on Saturday." I wondered what the story would be this time.

On one Tuesday morning as I was driving Mungai to school, we said our morning prayer in the car. Then he told me that Jesus had just spoken to him and said, "Mungai, you shall visit heaven again on Saturday."

I wondered what the story would be this time.

On that Sunday morning, as soon as Mungai woke up, I asked him about heaven because I could remember that Jesus had promised him a visit.

"Jesus came and picked me up from the bed. We went up and up, viewing the planets. Mnjala was there too."

"What did you do in heaven?"

"When we got to heaven, we went upstairs where God is and we started to talk to him."

Mungai told God, "I want to do well in school."

God the Father replied, "It shall happen."

Next, Mungai told God, "I want you to give Mum a new job where she would not be travelling."

God answered again, "It shall happen."

As I write this book, God has already answered both of these requests. Mungai improved in school, and I got a new position at work where I do not have to travel. Praise God for this. It was miraculous how I got the position, and I thank God because it was His doing.

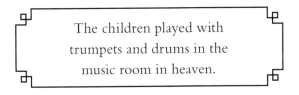

The children played with trumpets and drums in the music room in heaven.

After this conversation with the Lord, they were taken to the music room in heaven where they found many types of instruments made out of gold. Mungai said there were drums, trumpets, guitars, flutes, and many others. The children played with the trumpets and the drums. Mungai said it was so much fun. I also talked to Mnjala that morning, and his story corresponded with Mungai's.

It is most certain that God loves to be worshipped in singing and in music. That must be the reason there is the music room in heaven. Wouldn't it be fun to play instruments in heaven to God our Father? "Praise Him with the sounding of the trumpet, praise Him with the harp and lyre, praise Him with tambourine and dancing, praise Him with the strings and flute, praise Him with the clash of cymbals, praise Him with resounding cymbals" (Ps. 150:3–5).

When they finished playing in the music room, they went out to play with kites. They said that many people were outside playing with kites, including Uncle Ken, who they saw again in heaven. He told me that Uncle Ken was very happy in heaven.

Then they swam in the water with many multicolored fish.

"The fish are not scared of us, and we can also breathe underwater when we are in heaven," Mungai repeated.

He seemed very happy to swim in heaven with these beautifully colored fish.

"So how did you get back home?" I asked my son.

He recounted to me how Jesus gave them two golden parachutes, which he instructed the boys to pull on the right side. They gently came down to earth as Jesus watched over them from heaven. Mungai said that, once he reached the window of his bedroom, the parachute disappeared. He entered the room. I was so fascinated by the fact that God used different means to bring them back home every other time. Evidently, Mungai never seemed scared of anything. He had come to love and trust Jesus completely.

God Closes the Mouths of People

It had been quiet for over three weeks. I wondered whether this was it, that God had said what He needed to say, and that now it was up to us to tell it to others. There had to be a reason why it had to be us, our home, and our lives. Because God's ways are not our ways and His thoughts are not ours, we cannot completely comprehend His purposes.

Another surprise was awaiting us on February 21, 2010. We woke up to a bright and beautiful Sunday. Mungai let me know that he had visited heaven again. He said he was with his cousin and they had just met in space and started touching the planets. Mungai said that Jesus was watching them from heaven. They knew they were very safe. God allowed them to touch all the planets, including planet Earth.

"We moved it a little bit because God allowed us to," Mungai said.

I wondered. He simply could not have made all this up. Moreover, the fact that Mnjala had the same story could not have been a coincidence. These two little boys do not have such ingenious minds to make up such incredible stories. I simply had to believe their story. I hope you believe it, too. It sounds impossible when you try to reason with your mind, but so does everything else in the Bible.

Either science or logic cannot explain many stories in the Bible. For example, how did Jonah stay in the stomach of a whale for three days without getting digested? How did the wall of Jericho fall after the Israelites went around it seven times? How did Abraham and Sarah get their son Isaac at age one hundred and ninety, respectively? What about the ten plagues in Egypt? How did the Red Sea part in the middle so the Israelites could cross over? What about Daniel in the den of lions? How could Shadrach, Meshach and Abednego survive in a fiery furnace? How did Jesus walk on water and feed five thousand people with two pieces of fish and five loaves of bread? How did He heal the sick by speaking healing to them? Most incredibly, how did Jesus rise from the dead? Well, that tells you and me that God is able to do all things. He has done it for these children. He has proven Himself supreme. He is God the King, the Maker of everything, all the living creatures, and all the hosts of angels. He created all these and can do anything. He made science, matter, energy, and time.

Mungai said they eventually entered heaven through a window and went up to where God was. He told them they would return to heaven again some other time. He then began to teach them.

He told them, "I, God, punish people who do not believe the words I have spoken to them."

He said that God told them that He can close someone's mouth such that he or she cannot talk or laugh. I remembered the story of Zechariah and how he was dumb for nine months. Zechariah, who is recorded as a being a priest in the Bible, is the father of John the Baptist. He and his wife Elizabeth had no children because his wife was barren. When they were well advanced in years, an angel of the Lord appeared to Zechariah in the temple and announced to him that he and Elizabeth would have a son. Zechariah doubted this word because of their old age, and he was struck mute because of his unbelief. I told the story to Mungai.

Mungai told me, "Mum, God always says the truth."

After God finished explaining this, the children were allowed to play with the kites and to swim. Mungai said their pajamas turned into swimsuits.

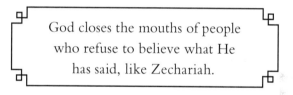

God closes the mouths of people who refuse to believe what He has said, like Zechariah.

Zechariah asked the angel, "How can I be sure of this? I am an old man and my wife is well along in years." The angel answered, "I am Gabriel. I stand in the presence of God, and I have been sent to speak to you and to tell you this good news. And now you will be silent and not able to speak until the day this happens because you did not believe my words, which will come true at their proper time" (Luke 1:18 –20).

After this visit to heaven, Mungai said they returned home on their own. Jesus watched over them from heaven.

"We were flying, Mum, very fast," he said with such thrill in his voice.

When Mungai got home, he entered through the roof of our bedroom, and he noticed me fast asleep on my bed. Mnjala also recounted the same story and said he entered their house through a closed door. He saw his mummy fast asleep in her bed. On this particular night, both their fathers were not home.

That afternoon, I was preparing dinner in the kitchen, and Mungai told me that Jesus was there in the kitchen with us. I knelt down right there and prayed.

Chapter 11

Mnjala's Story

On March 28, 2010, my sister Janet called me and said that Mnjala had just told her something very incredible. He told her that he was in heaven and Jesus had baptized him. He narrated how Jesus had held him and gently lowered him into a pool of water in heaven. That morning, he woke up very excited. He told his mother that Jesus told him to go to the kitchen where his mother was and tell her of his experience. His mother was indeed making breakfast in the kitchen.

Only God knows why he did this particularly with Mnjala because it has never happened to Mungai. In *We Saw Heaven*, Roberts Liardon narrates how he was only eight years old when he visited heaven. He, too, was baptized in heaven. "Then Jesus did something that is quite personal and extremely precious to me. I love to tell this part of the story. The Lord Jesus, the Holy Son of God, reached over and dunked me under the water of the river of life."[3]

---

3   Liardon, *We Saw Heaven*, 2000.

The remarkable thing I have noticed about Mnjala is that he really loves Jesus and trusts in Him completely. Anytime he visits my home and I ask that we pray, he will be the first one to close his eyes and the ever so eager one to read his Bible. He is a very gentle and calm child. He does not anger quickly; neither does he provoke other children to anger. Mnjala is also very bright in school. He is the youngest pupil in his class, yet he leads in all the subjects. As I mentioned earlier, from about the age of three, he was already telling his mother and sisters about visits with Jesus.

Some of the earlier stories I remember include a time when thieves wanted to break into their home. As the thugs were busy looking for an entry point into their home through the fence, Mnjala's two older sisters, Nzingo and Mary-Jane, got into a panic. It was around eight in the evening, and their parents were still at work. His sisters and the nanny were screaming and running around the house looking for the panic button. They were very afraid, but Mnjala sat calmly in front of the television set.

"Do not worry. The thieves cannot enter our house. Can't you see that Jesus is standing at the door?"

They wondered what he was talking about because they could not see Jesus, but sure enough, no thief entered their home. As suddenly as they came, the thieves left and fled at great speed without taking anything from their compound.

On another occasion while still a very young child, Mnjala told his mum that he could see angels guarding at their gate. "Mum, I usually see angels at our gate, but I sometimes do not see them."

One day, Mnjala's mum was seated in the living room reading, and Mnjala kept looking out of the window to see the angels. His mother tried to look, but she could see nothing but their lifeless black gate gazing back at her.

Shortly, Mnjala started waving at the angels. "Mum, they are waving back."

His mother was amazed, and so was I when I heard the story. This was way before my son began seeing angels.

I have already narrated that the first time my son had an encounter with angels that he was together with Mnjala. This was the time when they saw Angel Michael and Angel Gabriel guarding our gate with fiery swords in their hands.

One morning, at about the age of four, Mnjala told his mother that Jesus had come to his room during the night and had carried him on His lap. Then he asked his mother whether she knew that Jesus had holes in His hands. He said that he had touched the holes. He surprised his mum by saying that Jesus was crying. He was crying so much that he also cried with Him.

Janet, Mnjala's mother, asked, "Why was Jesus crying?"

"Jesus was crying because people do not believe in Him."

Another time, Mnjala told his mother that Jesus said he would use children to spread his word because adults were too busy making money.

A few months later, Mnjala said he saw a very big cross on the ground. Jesus was right there next to him. Jesus asked him to carry the cross, and when he tried to lift it, he could not. It was too heavy. Immediately, Jesus came near him and helped him carry this cross. It was possible to carry it because it became lighter.

Then Jesus asked, "Mnjala, you will carry my cross."

I believe this was the beginning of Mnjala's calling. His mother was not keeping a diary so I do not have the exact dates when these events took place. When my son began going to heaven with his cousin, it became a whole new story that led me to start keeping a diary.

> "Jesus was crying because people
> do not believe in Him."

One time, Mnjala's mother recounted to me how her son told her that he had asked Jesus for a blanket because it was very cold at night. It had rained very heavily, and their house had gotten really cold. Mnjala asked Jesus to keep him warm, and he said Jesus came and covered him with something like a blanket, which was so warm and nice. He added that he had felt so comfortable and slept so well. It got me thinking about how this young child had come to trust Jesus so much to the extent that, instead of going to his parents' room and asking for an extra blanket, he chose to ask Jesus to keep him warm. How awesome! He was probably about four years old at the time.

Mnjala's Dad Delivered from an Addiction

From the tender age of four, Mnjala had been asking his dad to stop smoking. He had consistently told his father that, if he did not stop smoking, he would get cancer and die. Mbugua, his dad, was addicted to cigarettes. He had been smoking for over fifteen years and attempted to stop smoking on several occasions, but he had found it impossible to quit the habit. Now his young son was pestering him about it every day.

After several vain attempts, Mnjala told his dad, "I am going to report you to Jesus!"

His dad simply ignored the threat; after all, this was just a little boy's talk. A few weeks later, Mbugua woke up with a very bad cold. He asked his wife Janet if he could smoke in the bedroom as he was feeling terribly weak and could not go outside. She agreed. He lit his cigarette and took the puff that became his final one. To this day, he says smoking was the most disgusting habit he had ever engaged in. The cigarettes he had enjoyed for so many years suddenly smelled like poo. He could not believe that he had smoked for all those years. He proceeded to throw away all his cigarettes that day and has never touched another ever since.

Nowadays, he cannot even stand the smell of cigarettes and excuses himself whenever others are smoking around him because he can still smell the poo from that last day he smoked. Basically, God showed him what a disgusting habit smoking is. He has now been set free! Since quitting the habit, he looks better, has put on some weight, and does not smell of cigarette smoke. We are all glad. God's Word, the Bible, says that our bodies are the temple of His Holy Spirit. This means we need to take care of our bodies because what we take in affects our health.

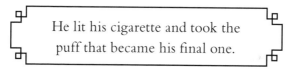

He lit his cigarette and took the puff that became his final one.

If you have any kind of addiction, ask Jesus to help you. He is the only one who can. Mnjala's father did not do it by his own strength but by God's help. He had tried by his own strength but failed. Trust in Jesus today and forever more.

Following Instructions

During the April school holidays, Mnjala had come over to our house for a couple days. On one of the mornings, the boys woke up rather late, and when they did, they quickly ran over to my room. They jumped onto my bed, I casually asked, "Did you go to heaven?"

"Yes." They answered in unison. "Jesus came to our bedroom to get us."

Mungai revealed, "Jesus held our hands, and then we left through the roof. We passed the planets, and then we entered heaven. I saw John the Baptist again. Then we swam in heaven, and I was wearing a green swimming costume. Mnjala was wearing a blue costume, and I went to the open and closed slides. I saw many angels."

"The closed tunnels for the slides are not dark because everywhere in heaven has light." Mungai attempted to put me into the full picture. "We had so much fun!"

"We had fun!" Mnjala echoed after Mungai. They both giggled, amazed at how heaven is fun-filled.

"How did you return home?"

"Jesus gave us gold-colored parachutes. He gave us instructions on how to use them. The parachutes had three buttons. One was for increasing speed, the next one was for going through objects. The third one was for coming to a stop." Mungai explained.

So they came down slowly with the golden parachutes using the three buttons as instructed with the planets in full view.

Jesus had also told them, "Mungai and Mnjala, be good to each other."

I was glad that Our Jesus had spoken to them about this because they had been naughty throughout the week, fighting for toys and pushing each other. The truth is that nobody is perfect. We all need Christ Jesus to give us direction and purpose. My son is just your regular child. He plays with all kinds of toys, he watches cartoons, and he has many friends and cousins with whom he enjoys playing with. He goes to school, does his homework, and so on. His dad and I have a responsibility to discipline him and to bring him up in the fear of God. So do Mnjala's parents and all the parents of this world. The Bible says we should teach our children His Word so they will not depart from it when they are grown.

I noticed that, after this visit, the two boys were really behaving themselves. They love Jesus, and they respect His authority. I can see and hear it from their conversations.

"When the parachutes had safely brought us back home, they just disappeared. Puff! Like that." Mungai made this sound as the two boys ran out of my room to go and play.

They left me in bed in total wonder, mulling over what they had just said, oblivious of the magnitude of their experiences.

My son, being a child, does not fully understand this great calling yet. He continually tells me that going to heaven is a normal thing for him. He is so used to it that he does not understand our excitement each time he tells us something. Most of the time, he explains something and then goes off to play, leaving us in total amazement.

Jesus at a Get-Together

One Saturday afternoon, during the same April holidays, my friend Zenah asked me and the boys to go and talk about heaven to a group of about fifteen teenage girls who were visiting her. At about 3:00 p.m., while we were on our way to her house, the boys mentioned that Angel Michael was in the car with us, seated in the backseat between them. I was so thrilled that I just praised the Lord. God had obviously sent His angel to take charge over us.

We arrived at Zenah's apartment and shared a number of experiences the boys had from their trips to heaven. During the session, the boys casually mentioned to the group that Jesus was right there in the middle of the living room. We were all, to say the least, amazed!

Zenah suggested that, because the Lord was present, it was in order for the girls to make their prayer requests known to Him. A few girls dared to ask Jesus what was in their hearts at the time, and each received an audible answer from Jesus through the mouths of Mungai and Mnjala. One particular girl, Irene, asked Jesus to heal her of acute ulcers, and she has since been completely healed.

Another girl, Abigail, asked Jesus whether her brother who had travelled to Turkey was safe because it had been over a year since the family had received any news from him. Jesus responded that the brother was well. But even better still, this brother has since returned home for holiday as I write this book.

A third girl, Brenda, asked Jesus whether her older sister would be able to travel to work in Dubai, which is in the United Arab Emirates. At the time, the UAE had imposed impossible visa conditions on every Kenyan travelling to their country due to some differences between the two governments. Jesus responded that her sister would go to work in Dubai. Seven months after Brenda received the positive response, her sister left to work in the UAE. She not only found a job, but she had all her expenses paid, including airfare and accommodation.

Another girl asked the Lord whether she should serve Him in the Catholic or Protestant church. To this question, the Lord responded Protestant through the children. This girl was particularly concerned about where to serve the Lord because, since getting saved, she was not comfortable with the rituals in the Catholic church, and this had brought her problems with her family. She no longer believed in the recitation of the rosary because she now believed that God was her only mediator and intercessor, as it is clearly written in 1 Timothy 2:5–6. "For there is one God and one mediator between God and men, the man Christ Jesus, who gave Himself as a ransom for all men - the testimony given in its proper time." Moreover, her faith had also changed in regards to the practice of confession because she had come to learn that she could confess her sins directly to God because He hears us. One does not have to keep his or her sins until the day of confession before a priest. She wanted to be sure about what God wanted for her life. Now she had received an answer directly from Jesus Himself.

Many of the girls have confessed that their lives have been changed since hearing the stories about heaven. It brought the reality of Christ Jesus and His love for us to their attention.

Chapter 12

Mansions in Heaven

On the evening of April 25, 2010, Mungai reported how Jesus had shown him many houses in heaven. He described them excitedly.

"Mum, they are many houses in heaven. Very many. I could not count them. I am thinking there were billions. They are so big and many. Some look like apartments, and I saw Uncle Ken in one of the houses. He was looking at me through a big window, and Jesus was in the window above Uncle Ken. The windows were so big. Mum, these houses are too many. And they are so beautiful. They are shining. They are made out of gold."

When Mungai told me about the mansions in heaven, what stuck in my heart was the word "many." He kept repeating that word until I remembered the verse in the Bible where Jesus talks about there being many rooms in His Father's house. In some versions of the Bible, they have used the word "mansions" instead of "rooms."

"Do not let your hearts be troubled. Trust in God, trust also in me. In my Father's house are many rooms; if it were not so, I would have told you. I am going there to prepare a place for you. And if I go and prepare a place for you, I will come back and take you to be with me that you also may be where I am. You know the way to the place where I am going" (John 14:1–4).

> "There are many houses in heaven, Mum. Very many. I could not count them. I am thinking that there were billions."

There is no doubt that God has prepared a beautiful place for us. We have no reason to doubt that. God's Word is true. It has been tried and tested. How could these children have seen something that is exactly like what is described in the Bible? As we have read earlier, they do not have dreams. They actually go to heaven in their spirits. In fact, even science would tell you that no two people could perceive the world in the same way, let alone have the exact same dreams. So even if these children were dreaming, it is utterly impossible for them to have the same dreams. Also surprisingly, these boys have each told us that they do not wish to return home when they are in heaven. Heaven is a place full of happiness and peace because of the presence of God Almighty.

Jesus Promises That I Will Visit Heaven

On Monday May 24, 2010, Mungai did not go to school as he was not feeling very well. As I was driving off to work, he told me that Jesus had visited at night.

"Mum, He stood near your wardrobe, and your clothes were shining."

"Did Jesus say anything to you?" I asked.

"Jesus said, 'Hi, Mungai.'"

This was the second time that Mungai had said that he saw my clothes shining in the wardrobe. I have often wondered what this means. Some people have suggested that it could mean that God's glory is upon me. Because of this, I feel a responsibility to share His Word with those who do not know Him. My prayer is that I do not disappoint Him.

Later in the day, I telephoned Mungai, and he told me that Jesus was in my bedroom with him. Mungai was watching cartoons, and Jesus was seated on the black leather chair in our room, watching over him.

"Mum, the chair does not even look black. It is shining so much because Jesus is on it."

"Tell Jesus that I would like Him to take me to heaven."

Mungai said, "Jesus can hear you, and He said yes."

I was very excited to hear this but quite anxious as well.

In the evening when I got home, Mungai said, "Jesus is right here with us."

So I asked directly, "Jesus when I am going to heaven?" My heart was beating very fast, wondering how Jesus was going to respond.

Mungai responded, "Jesus has said that, the next time I go to heaven, you will be there, too."

"When will this happen?"

"It will take place after the wedding we are attending on Saturday."

This answer surprised me so much. My heavenly visit was going to take place so soon. Now that I had the answer, I wondered how it was going to happen, how I was going to go, what I would see, and what I would say to God. I did not feel worthy of Him, worthy to be in His holy presence.

On Sunday morning, the morning after I was supposed to have gone to heaven, I woke up beautifully. I felt like a little baby. I felt like I had slept so soundly. I had never felt this way before. It felt strange that I had woken up at the same time with Mungai, but I could not remember being in heaven. I could not even remember dreaming. I am usually a very dreamy person, but on this particular day, I could not remember having dreamt. I just felt so well rested and calm. I went downstairs to make breakfast, but I kept wondering what could have happened. Jesus cannot say something and not fulfill it. I hoped that something would jolt my mind to remember as the day went on.

We got ready and went to church. On our way home from church, Mungai exclaimed, "Jesus is in the car with us."

"Ask Him why I did not go to heaven."

Then Mungai answered me, very surprised, "But, Mum, you were in heaven. I saw you there!"

Our conversation ended there because Mungai saw his dad and ran to meet him. We were headed to my parents-in-laws' house for lunch, so I left this conversation for later. While there, I took advantage of the opportunity to share with my husband's relatives about the visions Mungai had. They were in awe, and so was I. Every time I talk about these experiences, I feel the presence of God surrounding me.

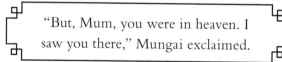

"But, Mum, you were in heaven. I saw you there," Mungai exclaimed.

When we returned home and were preparing for bed, I asked Mungai, "What did you mean when you said that you saw me in heaven? I cannot remember being in heaven."

He was a bit surprised that I could not remember. He touched my face and said, "You see, Mum, in heaven, the biggest room is where God is. It is called the throne room. Then the second-biggest room is the toy room, where we play. The third-biggest room is the library, where you were, Mum. 'The Library' is written on the door. You were seated on a beautiful carpet reading a golden Bible. Many books are in the library in heaven. There was also a big TV, which was showing TBN [Trinity Broadcasting Network], but you were not watching the TV. You were reading the golden Bible. Mum, those people preaching on TBN better know what they are saying because God is watching them."

"What was I wearing?" I asked Mungai.

"You were wearing something pink."

Oh, yes, that night I had gone to bed in a pink spaghetti top with pink and grey slacks! I thought to myself, *But what? I had actually visited heaven but could not remember a thing.* Mungai also told me that God had asked him and Mnjala to go and see what I was doing in the library in heaven. They peeped at me through a big window, but I did not look up at them. I could not remember being in heaven, but I believed what the children said. I thought about this for a long time. I could not understand why God had hidden this from me. He is all knowing, and He has my best interests in mind. It will be revealed in due time. I am sure of that.

The Twenty-Four Elders in Heaven

One day, as Mungai and I were making our way home from my parents' house, he asked me, "Mum, do you know some people in heaven who are called the twenty-four elders?"

This question totally stunned me. Whoever talks about the twenty-four elders? I am almost certain that most Sunday schools do not teach kids about these elders. A number of adults, even long-term Bible believers, have never heard of them.

God has certainly not finished surprising me, I thought to myself.

Anyway, my son said that God instructed him to sit on a beautiful, shiny, red sofa set and watch the twenty-four elders. "Mum, these twenty-four elders were just praising and worshipping God. They did not stop the whole day, and that is what they do the whole night. They were saying nice things to God. They told Him, 'You are marvelous. You are wonderful. You are holy. You are the Lord God Almighty.'"

"How were they dressed?" I asked.

He replied, "They were wearing white with golden crowns on their heads. They look like angels. They were even making circles as they praised God. Sometimes they would fly up and then down. Then they kneel before God."

I was totally astounded. When we got home, I got the Bible and opened to the book of Revelation. I knew I had read something about these twenty-four elders. I found it in Revelation 4, one of the rarest books read by believers because of its many visions and images mainly related to the end-times. My heart beat with excitement. I could hardly fathom yet again that what my son had just told me was right there before me, in the Bible, in God's Word.

> "The twenty-four elders say nice things to God all day and all night. They do not stop," Mungai narrated.

At once I was in the spirit and there before me was a throne in heaven with someone sitting on it. And the one who sat there had the appearance of jasper and carnelian. A rainbow, resembling an emerald, encircled the throne. Surrounding the throne were twenty-four elders. They were dressed in white and had crowns of gold on their heads. From the throne came flashes of lightning, rumblings and pearls of thunder. Before the throne, seven lamps were blazing. These are the seven spirits of God. Also before the throne there was what looked like a sea of glass, clear as crystal. In the center, around the throne, were four living creatures and they were covered with eyes, in front and in the back. The first living creature was like a lion, the second was like an ox, the third had a face like a man and the fourth was like a flying eagle. Each of the four living creatures had six wings and was covered with eyes all around even under his wings. Day and night they never stop saying: "Holy, holy, holy is the Lord God Almighty; Who was, and is, and is to come." Whenever the living creatures give glory, honor and thanks to Him who sits on the throne and who lives forever and ever, the twenty-four elders fall down before Him who sits on the throne and worship Him who lives forever and ever. They lay their crowns before the throne and say: "You are worthy, our Lord and God, to receive glory and honor and power, for you created all things, and by your will they were created and have their being" (Rev. 4:2–11).

Isn't this amazing! Indeed, the Lord is real, and He created everything. Mungai once mentioned to me that the words the "throne room" were written in gold in heaven, and that was why he knew the words the "throne room." He said this was where

God sat on a very big, white throne. He also told me that the throne room was very big because God was big, too. Mungai also said this throne room was in the center of heaven because that was what he had seen. He said he saw a compass that had all the directions: north, south, east, and west.

God Never Sleeps

One day, Mungai told me something very comforting. He said that God never falls asleep, that He is always watching planet Earth and the people He created. These were such powerful words coming out of a seven-year-old boy. "He will not let your foot slip—He who watches over you will not slumber; indeed, He who watches over Israel will neither slumber nor sleep" (Ps. 121:3–4).

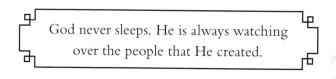

God never sleeps. He is always watching over the people that He created.

I find comfort in these words that God stays awake all the time. This means that nothing passes Him. Nothing happens without His knowledge. Every second of our lives, God is awake, brooding over us like a hen broods over her little chicks.

Do Not Worry

This next story I would like to share has changed my way of thinking and made me see God in a totally different light. I understood then that God is very big. Not only did He create the heavens, the earth, and everything in it, including all the people, He also cares about us deeply. God is love.

On this morning, my son woke up to tell me not to worry about anything. "Mum, you have to stop worrying."

His words startled me. "Why are you telling me to stop worrying?"

"God is so big, Mum, and there is nothing He cannot do for you."

He, still in his pajamas, was seated on his bed, and I was standing by the bed looking at him. He stretched out his hands to give a description of what he saw.

"God is so big, Mum. I saw Him seated in heaven, and His feet were here on earth!"

What Mungai said in his childlike language is what is written in God's Word in Isaiah 66: 1. "Heaven is His throne, and the earth is His footstool."

God cares about us more than anything else that He created. He even gave us dominion over everything. We are more precious to Him than we know.

> Therefore I tell you, do not worry about your life what you will eat or drink; or about your body, what you will wear. Is not life more important than food, and the body more important than clothes? Look at the birds of the air, they do not sow or reap or store away in barns, and yet your heavenly father feeds them. Are you not much more valuable than they? Who of you by worrying can add a single hour to his life? (Matt. 6:25).

God has also commanded us in His Word not to worry and instructed us to pray instead. He wants us to pray without ceasing. I have learned to rely on God for everything, and He has proven Himself faithful again and again. I thank Him that He has used my son to teach me this very important lesson in His Word, and now I can share it with others.

Do not be anxious about anything, but in everything, by prayer and petition, with thanksgiving, present your requests to God. And the peace of God which transcends all understanding will guard your hearts and your minds in Christ Jesus (Phil. 4:6).

A Gruesome Trip to Hell

On Sunday, June 13, 2010, my sister Janet visited us with her son Mnjala. They arrived at about 10:00 a.m. No sooner had they arrived, than the two boys excitedly ran upstairs to see Mungai's new toys that he had acquired recently. After a while, as I was preparing breakfast, the two boys came downstairs and began to narrate to us the strangest of stories. Mungai went first, saying they had been to hell that night with Jesus.

"Mum, in hell we saw people being beaten by demons. They were being beaten for nothing. They had not done anything, and the demons were beating them. They were beaten until they were bleeding. Then the demons were drinking their blood. You know there is no water in hell."

My sister and I were so stunned. We looked at each other and then back at the kids.

"What did the demons look like?' I asked the children.

"They looked like they have been made out of "pupu" and they had red eyes." Mungai answered.

Mnjala took over. "Aunty Lyee, the demons are very very big, and they have sharp claws."

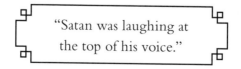

"Satan was laughing at the top of his voice."

"Then we saw Satan. He was laughing at the people who were being beaten," Mungai continued. "Satan was laughing at the top of his voice."

"How was Satan laughing?" Janet asked.

Mnjala let out a loud, eerie sarcastic laugh, "Ha! Ha! Ha! This is how he sounded."

Mnjala went on to describe the stench of hell. "Hell smells so bad. It smells like rotten garbage and many toilets that have not been flushed."

We laughed, but in my heart of hearts, I knew it was not so funny for those already in hell. "Mungai said, "I felt like vomiting while we were in hell, even just looking at the demons made me feel like throwing up."

As we were still going over the children's experience in hell, Mnjala surprised me by saying in a singsong voice, "Aunty Lyee, I saw you in heaven."

My sister Janet commented, "If they say they saw you in heaven, then they did."

I believed them, though again, like last time, I did not have a recollection of the experience. The children shared the story of hell in church later that morning. The congregation was dumbstruck, and so were we.

After church, while we were having lunch, I asked, "How does Satan look like?"

"He is so ugly; he is the ugliest thing I have ever seen." Mnjala replied.

"But his body was somehow beautiful because it had many colors like the rainbow. Jesus told us that Satan can change into different forms." Mungai added.

Mungai said, "He had one red eye and one white eye, and he had some marks on his nose. He had such a big mouth that we could not see his cheeks. He had many large teeth upwards and downwards. He also had horns on his head, and his hands were full of fingers."

"His head was full of snakes," they added.

> "Hell smells very bad. It smells like rotten garbage and many toilets that have not been flushed," Mnjala described the stench of hell.

"Were you boys scared?"

"No, we were not scared because Jesus was there with us. The devil and his demons could not see us. But afterwards, Jesus made light in hell which made Satan and his demons begin to run around in circles in great fear. They were wondering where they could hide from Him. Satan was very scared." Mungai informed us.

Yes, Satan is real, and so is hell. It is a place of torment for those who have rejected God. The devil is a deceiver, and he has deceived many that life is just here and now and heaven and hell do not exist. It has also been said that there is an in-between called purgatory, but this is a deception. You will not have another chance for people on earth to pray you into heaven when you have already died. You have to make the choice to accept Jesus Christ, the only way to heaven. Do not wait for another day because you do not know what tomorrow will bring. You do not know whether you will be alive tomorrow to have another chance to ask Jesus into your heart. He is knocking at the door of your heart. If you open it, He will come in and live in your heart. "And the devil, who deceived them, was thrown into the lake of burning sulfur, where the beast and the false prophet had been thrown. They will be tormented day and night forever and ever" (Rev. 20:10).

About Satan, the Fallen Angel

According to the Bible, Satan was an angelic being who God threw out of heaven. He was created with beauty, and he was the angel in charge of music. Thereafter, he became proud and wanted to be above God. He wanted to become God, so he was removed from the presence of God. Satan was created as a cherub, one of the angels that worship God. He is also known as Lucifer or the devil. He must have fallen from heaven some time before the creation of the world because he was present in the Garden of Eden where he tempted Adam and Eve.

> You were blameless in your ways from the day you were created till wickedness was found in you. Through your widespread trade you were filled with violence, and you sinned. So I drove you in disgrace from the mount of God and I expelled you, O guardian Cherub, from among the fiery stones. Your heart became proud on account of your beauty and you corrupted your wisdom because of your splendor. So I threw you to the earth; I made a spectacle of you before kings (Ezek. 28:15).

Since then, Satan was completely separated from God. He continues to rebel against God and does everything that opposes the Word and will of God. After his fall, Satan became the prince of the air and the ruler of this world. "Now is the time for judgment on this world, now the prince of this world will be driven out" (John 12:31).

Satan deceives, tempts, and accuses God's people. He uses everything in his power to take as many people as he can to hell because, for him, his fate has been sealed. He will eventually be thrown into the lake of fire with all those he has managed to deceive. Satan has used false religions, devil worshiping, cultic religions, witchcraft, and New Age religions to deceive many. The Bible says the devil has come to steal, kill, and destroy.

Satan steals people away from the kingdom of God. He has made many fall away from worshiping the true God. If you once knew God and then walked away, Satan has stolen you. This means that you no longer belong to God but to Satan. Satan is in the business of stealing people from God. He does not care about the ones who are not in God because they are already his. You need to be aware of his schemes.

Satan kills by taking you away from spiritual awareness. One dies in the spirit once Satan has gotten hold of you. You become blind to the things of God such that you reject Him whenever anyone tries to tell you about God. You become dead spiritually, and Satan continues to keep you in this state until he is able to kill you physically so you do not have an opportunity to repent and go to heaven.

Satan destroys life. Once he has stolen you and killed your spiritual awareness, he simply starts to destroy your life. He can use anything to do so. He could lure you into alcoholism, drug addiction, sexual addiction, prostitution, pornography, among other things. He can get you into cultic churches, the occult, witchcraft, and many other satanic-oriented activities. He is a schemer and has many ways of destroying your life.

The word of God says the devil is like a roaring lion roaming around looking for someone he can devour. Do not let that someone be you. The Bible also says that, if you resist the devil, he will flee from you. You cannot resist the devil on your own. You need to be under God's authority, under His protection, so as to be able to put up a resistance against the devil.

"Submit yourselves, then to God. Resist the devil and he will flee from you. Come near to God and he will come near to you" (James 4:7).

God Tested Me

One Monday evening as I was putting Mungai to bed, he said he saw me in heaven again. "Mum, you were in the library in heaven again. Mnjala and I were looking at you through a window. We saw you reading a golden Bible, and you were also watching a big TV."

I was shocked to hear about this once more. I simply could not remember being in heaven. "What was I wearing?" I asked.

"You were wearing a yellow outfit that had golden stars on it, and the stars were glittering. You were lying on your stomach like this." He lay on his stomach on my bed. "And you were playing with your legs like this." He moved his legs up and down.

I was in total amazement and speechless. I wondered, *How does God want to use me?*

"Mum, you were reading a little then watching the television."

"Did I look at you and Mnjala or say anything?"

"No, you did not. We looked at you for a few minutes and then we went to the toy room."

"What did you do there?" I asked.

"We played with many nice toys. There were some skateboards that fly when you ride on them, even cars. You sit on them, and they fly."

What fun! That's exactly what a child would wish a real toy could do.

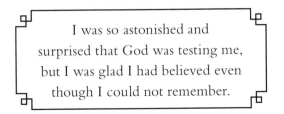

I was so astonished and surprised that God was testing me, but I was glad I had believed even though I could not remember.

Just before we went to bed a day in June, I asked Mungai, "Did you go to heaven last night? I had posed this same question to him earlier and he had told me to wait until later.

"Yes, I went to heaven with Mnjala and God told us that He was very happy with you because you believed that we saw you in heaven even though you could not remember."

Mungai concluded, "God told us that He was testing you, and He was so happy that you had believed."

The Bible records in the book of John that God is happy with those who believe in Him without seeing Him. "Then Jesus told him, 'Because you have seen me, you have believed; blessed are those who have not seen and yet they have believed'" (John 20:29).

I was so astonished and surprised that God was testing me, but I was glad I had believed even though I could not remember. Dear reader, God exists. He has revealed Himself through His Word, the Bible.

Then I asked Mungai, "After God talked to you, what else happened in heaven?"

"God told us to go to Uncle Ken's house. We found him seated on a chair with his legs crossed and he was reading a newspaper about the planets."

"How does Uncle Ken's house look in heaven?" I asked.

"It is very big, and it has beautiful furniture and pictures inside."

"Whose pictures?"

"The biggest picture is of Jesus and then other people in heaven like Moses."

I instantly realized the stories had become more detailed and much bigger. We had moved from seeing angels, visits by Jesus, and visits to heaven and hell to much more. The visit to hell, for instance, was very detailed. The boys had actually seen Satan and the dreadful torments of hell. In their visits to heaven, they had now seen the twenty-four elders and the numerous mansions, and God was deliberately teaching them from His mighty throne. What a journey!

It is evident that God has more in store for us. He is not done yet. He is preparing these boys for some mighty things. I somehow seem to be in the picture enough for God to put me through a test. Throughout God's Word, the Bible, we see God testing His people. God tests His children in order to produce good fruit. "Consider it pure joy, my brothers, whenever you face trials of many kinds, because you know that the testing of your faith develops perseverance. Perseverance must finish its work so that you may be mature and complete, not lacking anything" (James 1:2–4).

God tested Abraham by promising him that he would be a father of many nations, yet his wife Sarah was barren, and the two of them were well advanced in years. Everything seemed against this dream, but God eventually gave them a son named Isaac when Sarah was ninety and Abraham was one hundred years old. Even after giving Abraham a son, God asked him to sacrifice this son on a mountain. What a testing this was! Abraham believed God and proceeded to the mountain to sacrifice his promised son, Isaac. But God intervened and spoke to Abraham not to harm the child, and He immediately provided a lamb to sacrifice in the place of his son because Abraham passed the test. Isaac thereafter got two sons named Jacob and Esau. Then Jacob bore twelve sons, who became the lineage of the tribe of Israelites. Thus, God fulfilled His promise to Abraham to make him a father of many nations.

The testing continued with the Israelites who entered into slavery in Egypt under a very oppressive ruler. Eventually, God set them free from Pharaoh's hands, but Pharaoh later pursued them into the desert. The Israelites began to doubt God's salvation because of the mighty Red Sea before them. God parted the sea in order for them to cross over on dry land. Pharaoh and his Egyptian army were destroyed in the waters of the Red Sea when the waters that had formed a wall came back to normal after the Israelites were safely across.

While in the desert, they had many instances when God tested them. God is in the business of testing His people in order for us to learn how to trust in Him.

Chapter 13

The Newspaper in Heaven

> God had written, "These
> are my messengers, and they
> have been visiting heaven."

The following day, just before bedtime, Mungai told me something very interesting. A newspaper in heaven contained a picture of him and Mnjala in the children's section. God had asked the two boys to go and visit Uncle Ken in his mansion. They found him seated cross-legged on a beautiful sofa, reading a newspaper. Uncle Ken showed them an article with their photos in the newspaper in heaven. I was most surprised to hear that there are newspapers in heaven.

Mungai said they saw their full pictures with their three names, and God had written, "These are my messengers, and they have been visiting heaven."

Mungai said, "Our three names, Mungai Mnjala Waiyaki and Baraka Mnjala Mbugua."

Beneath the article were stories about the planets. I was so amazed. Mungai explained that God tells the angels to write the newspapers, which they deliver to each house for everyone to read. Mnjala had already told his mother this story, which I learned from my telephone call to them later that day. Mungai also reported that they appeared photographed in their pajamas in heaven's newspaper. I was overjoyed!

This means that everyone in heaven knows that God is using these children to spread the gospel of Jesus Christ. I have wondered about our other relatives who died in Jesus, if they remember our children and us. I thought of my Grandmother Grace, who loved Jesus with all her heart and always prayed for her family's salvation. Isn't she ecstatic to read in heaven that her great-grandsons are visitors in heaven and they are going to be preachers? No wonder heaven is a place of inexplicable joy. May God's will be done on earth as it is in heaven!

Twelve Is a Special Number to God

On Saturday, June 26, 2010, as we were driving to the barbershop, I was pondering in my mind about when some of the things God had promised to do in Mungai's life would happen. It was as if God were reading my mind because, no sooner had I begun to ponder about these things, than Mungai said that God had just spoken in his heart and said they would happen when he was twelve years old. Twelve is a very special number to Him. Indeed, we see the number twelve recorded in many instances in the Bible. Jesus was twelve when he first went to church, Jesus had twelve disciples, Jacob had twelve sons, and there were also the twelve tribes upon which the nation of Israel was founded. "When he was twelve years old they went to the Feast according to the custom" (Luke 2:42).

He appointed twelve—designating them apostles—that they might be with Him and that He might send them out to preach and to have authority to drive out demons. These are the twelve he appointed: Simon (to whom he gave the name Peter), James son of Zebedee and his brother John (to them he gave the name Boanerges, which means Sons of Thunder), Andrew, Philip, Bartholomew, Matthew, Thomas, James son of Alphaeus, Thaddaeus, Simon the Zealot and Judas Iscariot, who betrayed Him (Mark 3:14–18).

That God will fulfill His promises concerning Mungai when he turns twelve is really up to Him. Only He knows how this will happen. He made everything and can do anything. He is the giver of all good things. His ways are not our ways; neither are His thoughts our thoughts. As far as heaven is from the earth, so are His ways and thoughts far above ours. We cannot compete with our Maker. I have submitted everything to Him.

Angel Michael and Angel Gabriel

In the morning of August 1, 2010, I asked Mungai whether he had gone to heaven, and he said he did, but he would tell me about it later. Just like any other child his age, he was busy watching cartoons and did not want to be distracted. I had also noticed that he was so used to going to heaven that he would say that he found it normal. For me, this would never be normal, but maybe it's because I am an adult. Anyway, I went downstairs and made breakfast for the two of us and my sister Jael, who was visiting. We talked and prayed with her, and we later got ready and went to church.

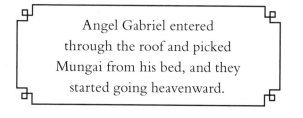

Angel Gabriel entered through the roof and picked Mungai from his bed, and they started going heavenward.

After church, Mungai and I had a meeting to attend at my parents-in-laws' home. We had planned to go in one car together with his Uncle Kinuthia and family. On our way to Uncle Kinuthia's house, Mungai narrated to me how he and Mnjala got to heaven that night. Mungai said that Angel Gabriel entered through the roof and picked him from his bed, and they flew heavenward. As they were going up, they met Mnjala and Angel Michael. They first went to see the planets, and then they all decided to race to heaven. Mungai told me that they all got to heaven at the same time because Angel Gabriel allowed the tie, even though he thought he is a faster angel given that God always sends him and he does everything very fast. God sends Angel Michael, on the other hand, to fight. They entered heaven through a window and went directly to the throne room where God was.

Then God greeted them with His big hand and told them, "Mungai and Mnjala, welcome to heaven."

After God the Father greeted them, they went off to the swimming pool. They later also played with the kites in heaven. Mungai's was red and white while Mnjala's was red and blue.

"Mum, we had so much fun in heaven," Mungai stated happily.

"How did you return home?" I posed my usual question.

"Angel Gabriel and Angel Michael brought us back. God has picked Angel Gabriel to watch over me and Angel Michael to watch Mnjala."

I wondered why God would assign these children such mighty angels. Could it be that they would face more attacks from Satan as they begin to minister God's message to the world?

Angels move at inconceivable speeds. They can move from one place to another at the speed of light. I am picturing them in my mind moving with these children at great speeds. Otherwise, how would they reach heaven in such a short period of time? And yes, angels operate in the spiritual realm, hence our inability to see them unless God allows us to.

Angel Michael has been described as an archangel in the Bible. In Daniel 12:1, Michael has been described as the great prince who protects. Michael is the commander of all the warring angels. He leads all the warring angelic hosts into battle against Satan and his demons. His name is a combination of Hebrew words that mean "Who is like God?"[4] Angel Michael is mentioned in the book of Daniel as the angel who went to rescue Angel Gabriel, who was carrying a message for Daniel from God, but the forces of evil had prevented him from delivering it promptly. Angel Michael helped push back the powers of darkness that were blocking Gabriel from delivering the message to God's servant. "But the Prince of the Persian Kingdom resisted me twenty one days. Then Michael one of the chief princes, came to help me, because I was detained there with the king of Persia" (Dan. 10:13).

Angel Gabriel has also many times been referred to as an archangel. Gabriel, whose name means "hero of God" or "warrior of God," is one of God's principal messengers.[5] God entrusted him to deliver incredible messages to Daniel, Mary, and Zechariah, as recorded in Daniel 8:16 and 9:21 and Luke 1:18–19 and 28–36. Both Angel Michael and Angel Gabriel have been given rank and power above all other angels.

---

4   Hunter, *The Angel Book*, 1999,

5   Ibid.

"Zechariah asked the angel, 'How can I be sure of this?' I am an old man and my wife is well along in years.' The angel answered, 'I am Gabriel. I stand in the presence of God and I have been sent to speak to you and to tell you this good news'" (Luke 1:19).

These boys are leading an incredible life. Many times, I lack the words to express how I feel deep inside. I will forever be grateful that God chose my son and my nephew, just little boys, to confirm His truths to us. We all belong to God, so he decides. He knows what is best for each one of us. Praise the Lord forever!

Michael Jackson is in Hell

As we were on our way to Mungai's grandparents' home, Mungai started to tell us that he had seen Michael Jackson in hell. We were in the car together with Aunty Annie, Uncle Kinuthia, Ryan, and Trudy. We were all stunned. We began asking him questions.

"How did you know it was Michael Jackson?'

"Everyone in hell knows it is Michael Jackson burning in hell."

"When someone is with Jesus, they know everything. That is how I knew it was Michael Jackson."

"What was Michael Jackson doing?" Ryan asked.

"His whole body was on fire and he was burning and running around screaming at the top of his voice." Mungai informed us.

I knew my son was telling the truth. How could he have said such a thing just out of the blue? It was impossible for him to talk about someone we neither discussed at home nor whose music we listened to. In fact, by the time Mungai was relating this to us, Michael Jackson had been dead for over a year. Michael Jackson was a dominant popular music figure in the 1980s and early 1990s.

My son did not grow up in this generation, so he cannot boast of listening to or loving his music.

We felt sorry for the late pop icon, but at the same time, we acknowledged he might never have lived for Jesus when he was alive. His song *'Thriller'* contains lyrics pointing to some knowledge of the occult world.

About Demons

God commands us in His Word not to be involved with the spirit world through the occult and devil worshipping. Many people get involved in the occult knowingly or unknowingly and without realizing how dangerous it is. If one goes to a fortune-teller, medium, or palm reader or reads tarot cards, plays the Ouija boards, or gets involved in horoscopes or channeling, they automatically open a door to the demonic world. Many people get enticed into the occult without realizing how harmful it is. Demons gain access into their lives through such practices. Other avenues through which demons can gain entry into a person's life are yoga, feng shui, visualization, witchcraft, drugs, alcohol, divination, transcendental meditation, and necromancy.

> Let no one be found among you who sacrifices his son or daughter in the fire who practices divination or sorcery, interprets omens, engages in witchcraft, or casts spell, or who is a medium or spiritist or who consults the dead. Anyone who does these things is detestable to the Lord and because of these detestable practices the Lord your God will drive out those nations before you. You must be blameless before the Lord your God (Deut. 18:10–13).

When men tell you to consult mediums and spiritists who whisper and mutter, should not a people inquire of their God? Why consult the dead on behalf of the living? To the law and to the testimony! If they do not speak according to this word, they have no light of dawn (Isa. 8:19–20).

When Satan fell from heaven, he was thrown out together with other angels who were also rebellious against God. They ceased to be holy angels and became evil angels or demons. Satan rules demons. They worship him and do his bidding. They entice people to fall into sin and have the ability to possess or influence human beings. The Bible has several stories of people possessed by demons.

"While they were going out a man who was demon-possessed and could not talk was brought to Jesus. And when the demon was driven out, the man who had been mute spoke. The crowd was amazed and said, "Nothing like this has ever been seen in Israel" (Matt. 9:32–33). "Then they brought Him a demon-possessed man who was blind and mute and Jesus healed him so that he could both talk and see" (Matt. 12:22).

"When Jesus got out of the boat, a man with an evil spirit came from the tombs to meet Him. This man lived in the tombs, and no one could bind him anymore, not even with a chain. For he had often been chained hand and foot, but he tore the chains apart and broke the irons on his feet. No one was strong enough to subdue him" (Mark 5:2–4).

From these texts, it is clear that demons can cause certain physical impairments in people such as blindness, deafness, muteness, insanity, and even behavioral changes, such as personality disorders, depression or despair, aggression, antisocial behavior, or supernatural strength. This is not to say that, when one has any of these symptoms, a demon has possessed him or her, though it could be a possibility. In the verses above, the men in question were blind and mute and had extraordinary strength because of the evil spirits that had possessed them. We learn that these men's sufferings ended when Jesus came into the scene and commanded the demons to leave. They left immediately, just by His Word.

Demons are under the control of Satan, and they influence people to spread lies and deceit in order to thwart the kingdom of God. Their main goal is to defeat the church of Jesus Christ. The Bible warns us that we are in constant battle with Satan, the enemy of our souls, and he and his demons are constantly fighting us.

> Finally, be strong in the Lord and in His mighty power. Put on the full armor of God so that you can take your stand against the devil's scheme. For the struggle is not against flesh and blood, but against the rulers, against the authorities, against the powers of this dark world and against the spiritual forces of evil in the heavenly realms (Eph. 6:10–12).

The only source of escape from the power of Satan is through believing in Jesus Christ and the word of God, the Bible. One cannot get rid of Satan and his activities by his own strength but only through God and His Word. Always remember, so long as you believe in Jesus, you have more power than the devil. We are more than conquerors through Jesus Our Lord.

> *In Luke 10:19, Jesus said, "I have given you authority to trample on snakes and scorpions and to overcome all the power of the enemy; nothing will harm you."*

Dear reader, please do not consult any witch doctor or medium or get involved in any of the demonic activities that have been mentioned. These individuals actually use demons to exhibit the power they seem to have. For example, the mediums who act as a go-between the living and the dead are, in reality, contacting demons. Instead, consult the wisdom of God, as the Bible says.

Music and Devil Worship

Music is a very powerful tool. It appeals to the soul, where our emotions are received and expressed. That is why music can make us, sad, happy, apprehensive, relaxed, and excited, and it generally has the ability to manipulate our emotions. Music can enter our minds and hearts whether we are willing to listen to it or not. It goes directly into the subconscious part of our mind.

Music can also change the atmosphere of a place. We have seen or heard of people passing out or going into frenzy during musical concerts. Most people have experienced the atmosphere of reverence and peace during the praise and worship session in church services.

Remember that Satan was an archangel who God made to make music in heaven. However, since his rebellion, he uses all he has to bring God's people down and has long used music as a weapon to destruct many from the knowledge of Christ Jesus.

Heavy metal music, rock, pop, and hip-hop are ways in which Satan has used to distract and destroy God's people, both the young and old. This music encourages a spirit of rebellion against God such that its listeners become inclined to totally defy order, God's order. As they fill their souls with this music, they disobey God's commandments. The spirit of the Antichrist starts to reign in their minds. They start to worship Satan through this music, knowingly or unknowingly. The impact of such music is big because of the way it has the power to play in your mind for days on end. Have you ever listened to a song and the song refused to live your mind? Yes, such is the power of music!

The devil uses some musicians to make music that will cause ordinary people to worship him. These musicians have made pacts with Satan to gain fame and money in exchange of making music that will encourage the worship of Satan. They make music that spread messages that do not encourage a right living or godliness but instead perpetuate homosexuality, fornication, adultery, drugs, murder, idolatry, violence, lies, and fantasies, thus drawing people's hearts away from the things of God.

Pastor Craig Lewis of Ex-Ministries tells a story about a musician by the name of Kevin Thornton, a member of the famous group called Color Me Badd. This man and his group members had made a pact with the devil, and they had become very famous. What people did not know was that, behind the scenes, the group would dedicate their songs to Satan, and they would perform certain rituals before a big performance. Craig talks of a song that was a hit in the whole world. The goal of this song was to make young people lose their virginity, and this is exactly what happened when the group would sing the song on stage. The crowds of people would move to the song, seemingly hypnotized, and they would want to imitate the lyrics of the song. The song, '*I Wanna Sex You Up,*' became a hit around the world. What was shocking is that, after Kevin left the band, he had forty-two demons that were living inside of him as a result of serving Satan for years. It took Pastor Craig up to three days to cast every one of these demons out of Kevin. One of the demons had refused to leave because it had been 'sung' into Kevin's spirit, and the pastor had to play some godly worship music to get the demon defeated.[6]

---

6   G. Lewis, *The Truth About Hip Hop X-Ministries.*

This reminds me of the story in the Bible where Saul had an evil spirit that God had allowed to come and torment him. Saul requested that David play him the harp in order for the evil spirit to depart. Saul knew the Lord was with David. "Whenever the spirit from God came upon Saul, David would take his harp and play. Then relief would come to Saul; he would feel better and the evil spirit would leave him" (1 Sam. 16:23).

From the examples cited above, we see how music is powerful and how it can be used for evil. If you have been listening to such music, please stop and ask God to forgive and cleanse you. Ask Him to renew a right spirit within you. Do not allow Satan to influence you through music. Do not allow him to take you to hell like he did Michael Jackson. The power is in your hands to make the right choice today. Resist the devil, and he will flee from you.

Our Lord Jesus visited a group of seven youths from Columbia, and they were shown heaven and hell. In their vision of hell, they saw John Lennon. Do you remember him? Of course, he was one of the members of the famous Beatles. This man hated Christianity, and he constantly blasphemed the word of God. He was reported as saying that their group would become more famous than Jesus Christ. He is now in hell as a result of his rebellion against God Almighty.

There is also a famous group called Bone Thugs and Harmony, four young men who are constantly singing about death and murder. On one of the CD album covers, their faces are reflected in the form of skeletons depicting death. On the back of this particular CD, there are pictures of four demons, one on each corner, and a paragraph written backwards. I have come to learn that witches, even in the olden days, used backward writings to cast spells on people. For one to read such writings, you need to use a mirror to read them. When you do this, you speak the words into your soul, hence casting the spell on yourself. I cannot imagine how many people impart doom and death to their souls when they buy music from this group. Would you like your children to become rebellious against God? If not, please ensure that you know the kind of music they are listening to and advise them accordingly.

The demon of suicide overcomes many young people once they start listening to music that is constantly talking to them about death. A number of such youth have admitted to having suicidal feelings while others have sadly been found hanging by the neck in their bedrooms with this music playing loudly.

In the recent past, many musicians are getting into the occult, the secret society, satanic new world order, freemasonry, and the Illuminati. This is often in search of fame and money, and unfortunately, Satan, the father of all lies, has deceived them that he will give them everything even in the life after. We have all read about the end of Michael Jackson. He will be in hell for eternity. He gained the whole world but lost his soul. The torture in hell is not worth living this life for Satan.

Jesus said in Mark 8:36–37, "What good is it for a man to gain the whole world, yet forfeit his soul? Or what can a man give in exchange for his soul?"

All this is evidence that it is important to know what kind of music you are purchasing before doing so. It would be helpful to know the background of the musician and his or her lifestyle and beliefs in order to make an informed decision.

About Cartoons

On one particular day, I came across a story on the Internet at www.spiritlessons.com. The story is about a young girl of eighteen years from Ecuador called Angelica Zambrano. Jesus had also visited her and shown her hell and heaven. Her story is amazing. To begin with, this young lady was shown hell. I was glued to what she had to say. In one section of her story, she talked about seeing children in hell, which almost made my heart stop. While in hell, Angelica was shown a vision of a young boy and how he lived while still here on earth. This boy was eight years old and had spent most of his time watching cartoons. While watching a cartoon called *Ben 10*, an evil spirit entered him, making him very rude and disobedient to his parents.

One day, the boy was very angry with his parents, so he ran out of the house. A car hit him. He died, and he is now in hell burning and in torment. Not only is he burning in hell, but the *Ben 10* monsters are in hell with him, constantly tormenting him.

Ben 10 is a cartoon series that portrays a boy who wears a watch on his hand and is able to turn into different aliens using this watch. This watch is called an "omnitrix," and it contains some strange power that enables this young Ben to turn into several different, ugly-looking aliens. He then fights other aliens or evil people while he is in the form of an alien. He exhibits a lot of power and might. This cartoon is intriguing. I have watched it myself a couple times. Mungai and Mnjala also used to watch it every day, and they would look forward to the program. They even had all sorts of toys and clothing from this cartoon: alien toys, pens, posters, T-shirts, shorts, and the omnitrix watch. It seemed very cool to have stuff from this cartoon as it was and has been the "in" cartoon for a while now.

When I read about Angelica Zambrano and her vision of the boy who was being tormented by *Ben 10* aliens in hell, I was very frightened. I knew she was telling the truth. I told Mungai about her and what Jesus had shown her. Immediately, Mungai informed me that Jesus had spoken into his heart. "Mum, Jesus has said that that girl your mum is talking about is saying the truth about cartoons."

Indeed many times, I had thought there is something eerie about this cartoon and many others. I had also asked Mungai to stop watching *Bakugan* because it had themes similar to *Ben 10*. We got rid of all the *Bakugan* and *Ben 10* toys and accessories. Mungai was glad to do so because he had received the confirmation from Jesus.

On another day, Mungai was watching a cartoon called *Star Wars: The Clone Wars*. I had asked him not to watch it because it was weird and scary. One time as he was watching it, Jesus spoke to him and asked him not to watch it.

On a similar topic, Jesus told my son that even some movies have demons in them. He was told that a demonic spirit could possess one while watching some movies. This is a direct warning that we should beware of what we watch.

In this area of media, it is particularly important that parents be aware of what their children watch. Indeed, it may even be beneficial to reduce the watching of television and playing of video games to a bare minimum. Not all is bad, however, but parental control and involvement is required.

It is the responsibility of parents to bring up their children in the fear of God. The Bible, which is God's Word, has commanded parents to do so. "Train a child in the way he should go, and when he is old he will not turn from it" (Prov. 22:6).

Jesus also taught Mnjala about cartoons. One day, he was busy playing with his *Ben 10* omnitrix. He put it on and twisted it just the way *Ben 10* does in the cartoon program. As soon as he hit the omnitrix, to his surprise, a demon came out of it! Mungai and Mnjala have seen demons in hell on several occasions, so they know what they look like. So Mnjala started fighting with this demon. He removed the evil watch and stepped on the foul creature that had come out of it. His mother came to his room and found that he had smashed his omnitrix. He simply informed her that a demon had come out of it. Imagine what would have happened to Mnjala if the demon had entered him! Without a doubt, he would have become like the boy who young Angelica had seen in hell. Parents, be warned that the enemy, who is Satan, is using cartoons to harm your children. He wants to destroy them while they are still young and ultimately take them to hell. Dear parents, please warn your children. Do not live in ignorance now that you know the truth about cartoons. Do not put your children in harm's way. Teach them what is right and wrong.

On another day, Jesus visited Mnjala, and he was taken to hell where he saw many children burning. He reported to me that these children looked his age and above. Satan had made them look very ugly and frightening. He saw *Ben 10* aliens, *Bakugan*, and *Pokémon* demons beating up these children. They were screaming and crying out for help. Mnjala also narrated how he saw some children in cages. They were locked in two by two. What a sad story. If only the parents of these children had directed them in the ways of God.

> But if anyone causes one of these little ones who believe in me to sin, it would be better for him to have a large millstone hung around his neck and be drowned in the depths of the sea. Woe to the world because of the things that cause people to sin! Such things must come, but woe to the man through whom they come! (Matt. 18:6–7).

Lydia Chola-Waiyaki

About Halloween

During the Halloween season, we were surprised by what the Lord revealed to the children. In Kenya, many shopping malls start to decorate and advertise weeks before the celebration. Halloween parties are held in various large malls within the city. A few days before the day, we visited a big shopping mall located in Nairobi. We found the mall had been decorated with various scary objects, like vampires, skeletons, black-hooded creatures, designed pumpkins, demon-looking dolls, and so on. Every corner of the mall had something frightening waiting around the bend. We felt scared and disturbed by what was going on around us.

Mungai and Mnjala were with me. As we were heading to the play park, they told me that the place was crawling with demons. No wonder there was an atmosphere of fear and evil in this place. They described to me that each object had between four to ten demons hanging around and within it. There was no doubt that God did not want us to celebrate Halloween. It does not bring glory to God in any way whatsoever. We quickly left the mall and prayed for God's protection.

> Halloween (All Hallows' Evening, Halloween, or All Hallows' Eve) is a yearly holiday observed around the world on October 31. It was thought to have originated with the ancient Celtic festival of Samhain when people would light bonfires and wear costumes to ward off roaming ghosts. Mystery, magic, and superstition always fill this holiday. The tradition of dressing in costume for Halloween has both European and Celtic roots.

> On Halloween, which was on the onset of winter, it was believed that ghosts came back to the earthly world.

People believed they would encounter ghosts if they left their homes. So in order to avoid being recognized by these ghosts, people would wear masks when they left their homes after dark so the ghost would mistake them for fellow spirits. This eerie day incorporates traditions from pagan harvest festivals and festivals honoring the dead. Typical festive Halloween activities include trick-or-treating, attending costume parties, carving jack-o-lanterns, lighting bonfires, visiting haunted attractions, playing pranks, telling scary stories, telling fortunes, and watching horror movies.[7]

Dear readers, all these activities practiced on Halloween bring a lot of superstition, fear, and worry into one's life with them. You expose yourself to the devil and his wicked schemes. Remember that the evil one is roaming around to see whom he could devour. If you give him a loophole, he will surely take it and bring destruction to you and your family. "Be self-controlled and alert. Your enemy the devil prowls around like a roaring lion looking for someone to devour" (1 Pet. 5:8).

A Message for Pastor George

On August 14, 2010, we had an awesome time at the fiftieth wedding anniversary celebration of my parents-in-law. We came back home tired but content because we had a very exciting day. My parents-in-law have been very great parents to me. They know and love Jesus, and He has been the foundation of their marriage. They gave advice that a house built on a poor foundation does not stand and the Lord Jesus is this solid foundation. This was a good lesson for all of us to learn and apply. After that wonderful occasion, all my young nieces and nephews came to my place for

7   Wikipedia

a sleepover because their parents wanted to go out for dinner and continue with the celebration.

When we woke up that Sunday morning, Mungai was very excited because his cousins had spent the night with us. He is an only child, so any visitor is usually most welcome to stay over. We had breakfast and got ready for church. After the service, I asked Mungai to talk to Pastor George and tell him what he had seen in hell. Mungai told the pastor that he had seen Michael Jackson burning in hell. He also told him that Jesus cannot help the people in hell because they did not love Jesus when they were on earth. Then Mungai told Pastor George that Jesus had said that he is a very good pastor and He is very happy with him. Wow, this was incredible news! The pastor, who was together with his mother and me at the time, was all so excited when Mungai gave him this great news.

On our way back home from church, I asked Mungai, "Can you repeat the pastor's story to me?"

"Jesus asked me to sit on a golden seat in heaven, and He sat on another golden seat across me. Then Jesus told me, 'Your pastor, Pastor George, is a very good pastor, and I am very happy with him.'"

This also confirmed to me that the Lord wanted us in that church. He knows exactly why we are there and why we are under the pastoral authority of this particular pastor. Pastor George later confessed to me that He needed to hear those words from God. God knows our every need, and He can use anyone to help us out.

Chapter 14

In Heaven Again

On this particular day, we went to visit my mother, together with Mungai and his friend Kibet. We found Mnjala who was there too visiting his grandmother. My mother immediately served us lunch when we arrived. As we devoured the sumptuous meal, we updated Grandma on the children's visits to heaven and hell. Mnjala began to relate their experiences in hell and repeated how they had both seen Michael Jackson there.

He added that Satan told them that he was not happy that they were born, but Jesus commanded him to be silent to the point whereby he could neither talk nor move. I pondered about what the future of these children would be like that drove Satan to tell them that he wished they were not born.

The answer must be souls, I thought.

Many souls will come to know the Lord, and Satan is not happy that he will lose many to God.

Mnjala said to me, "We were in heaven last night and Jesus told us, 'Mungai and Mnajala, be good friends.'"

I asked him, "What else did you do in heaven?"

"We played with kites," the two boys resonated in unison.

The boys were just casually narrating these stories without realizing what impact they were having on us, the listeners. We hung onto their every word and were greatly encouraged and uplifted. We felt the reality of heaven and the importance of making it there. Even today, no matter what happens in my life, I encourage myself with God's Word and His promise of heaven.

It Rained!

On August 20, 2010, we had just come back from a walk with Mungai, and he told me that God told him that it was going to rain. I was stunned! Less than an hour later, the rain started pouring, accompanied by thunder and lightning. Mungai also informed me that the power was going to go off, and it did. I felt that God was making my son believe in Him completely. When God would say something to him, it would happen eventually. This story also reveals that God is in charge of everything, including the weather.

On that particular day, there had been no sign of rain at all, but suddenly there was rain and even thunder. This reminds me of the story in the Bible when Jesus calmed the storm. He spoke to the storm, and it obeyed Him.

> One day Jesus said to his disciples, "Let's go over to the other side of the lake." So they got into a boat and set out. As they sailed, he fell asleep. A squall came down on the lake so that the boat was being swamped and they were in great danger. The disciples went and woke Him saying, "Master, Master, we're going to drown!" He got up and rebuked the wind and the raging waters; the storm subsided and all was calm. "Where is your faith?" he asked His disciples. In fear and amazement

they asked one another, "Who is this? He commands even the winds and the water and they obey Him" (Luke 8:22).

Yes, Jesus is Lord. He is the true God who made everything. He made the heavens and the earth and everything in it. He can command the storm, and it will listen.

That Sunday, Pastor George asked Mungai to tell the church what he had been seeing and what the Lord had shown him. We talked about everything, including Michael Jackson being in hell. Mungai could remember his first visit to hell and how Jesus had shown them Goliath burning and suffering in hell. We were all so amazed at what the Lord was teaching us through children.

An Even Grizzlier Scene in Hell

We had just finished breakfast when Mnjala began recounting what had happened that night. I remembered how the children had come running into my bedroom just before we went to sleep the previous night and reported that Jesus was in their bedroom. He had appeared at the door, and then He disappeared. Now here was Mnjala, excitedly narrating this incredible story. I was just in utter shock as I watched him recount how their night had been. He said that Angel Michael and Angel Gabriel came for them.

"Angel Gabriel picked Mungai, and Angel Michael picked me," Mnjala explained with excitement. "We went up through the roof and continued upward toward heaven."

He paused to comment, "The planets look so good and they go around the sun."

"The sun is so big, Aunty Lyee," he added.

"How did you enter heaven?"

"We entered through a gate and went up some stairs directly to where God was seated. God asked us to sit on the golden chair. When we sat down, the chair became two chairs."

Then God said, "Mungai and Mnjala, be good cousins."

God thereafter told them that they could go and play. They played with their kites. Mnjala had a red one, while Mungai had a white one.

> "Satan kept beating his demons, asking them to worship him more and more. He was not getting enough," the boys narrated.

After this, Jesus took them to hell. Mnjala described the scene, saying they saw Satan seated on a black chair and about twelve demons surrounding him, worshiping him. He (Satan) kept beating the demons and asking them to worship him more and more. He was not getting enough. Satan then ruthlessly commanded his demons to go and get two evil people from Planet Earth. The demons left and quickly returned with a man and a woman. The two people were screaming and pleading with the demons not to throw them into the fire. The demons did not pay attention to their cries, but they proceeded to throw them in mercilessly. The two became like skeletons because of the fire. They continued to cry out for mercy, but nobody cared. Indeed, the Bible puts it very clearly. Satan has no mercy. His work is to steal, to kill, and to destroy. "The thief comes only to steal and kill and destroy; I have come that they may have life, and have it to the full" (John 10:10).

Mnjala explained that he also saw some people burning in cages, and Michael Jackson was in one of them. The demons were asking him to dance as they pushed him around, and it looked very painful. He was hopping up and down in agony.

Mnjala continued, "The demons kept telling him, 'Dance!'"

As he tried to dance from the demands of the demons, they would throw hot coals at his feet. Satan was laughing at him and all those people burning in hell. At this juncture, Mungai wanted to know why the demons were asking Michael Jackson to dance. I told him how Michael Jackson loved to dance while he was alive. He was a great singer and dancer.

Mnjala added, "Satan, demons, and hell smell very bad. It smells like rotten eggs, rotten garbage, and toilets, just anything that smells bad mixed together."

Mnjala also explained that many people in hell were hopping up and down with their feet burning from the fire in hell. He then said that Jesus made them bigger than the demons, making it possible for them to step on them. Mnjala added that he even stepped on Satan's black seat, and Satan was very scared of them. He was running around very scared when he saw Mnjala's leg coming down to step on his chair. He told them he wished they were not born. But Jesus silenced him, and he fell down and was weak. He could not even talk or move. Indeed, we have more power than Satan does. Praise the Lord! I kept thinking how intense these visions had become.

At about 8:00 that evening, I was downstairs making a cup of tea, and the boys ran down to me, saying Jesus was in the house and He was in my bedroom. I ran up with them and knelt down before the King of kings and Lord of lords. I wanted to thank Him and to present my list of prayer requests that I wanted answered. Jesus is the only one who has answers to our requests.

On 14 April 2012, we were surprised when Mnjala was taken to hell again by our Lord Jesus and shown Michael Jackson and

Whitney Houston. Mnjala said, "They were next to each other in terrible pain and torment. Six demons surrounded Michael Jackson and they were asking him to sing the song *'Thriller.'* They were telling him that it is their favorite song."

"Three of the demons had whips in their hands and they would beat Michael Jackson mercilessly. The other three had knives and they would stab him through the back." Mnjala sadly added.

"The demons were scary and ugly."

Mnjala described them as having skeleton heads that were on fire and black bodies. Fire was coming out through their skeleton eyes. As Michael cried out for help, Mnjala heard him say, "Those who are listening to my music will come to hell."

Mnjala continued to narrate, "Next to Michael Jackson was Whitney Houston who was also being tortured by demons." Jesus was with Mnjala and so he was able to recognize the singer who had just died a few weeks earlier.

"She was also being beaten by demons. They were asking her to sing but she could not sing. Her voice was ugly as she tried to sing. The demons were laughing at her."

"What else was happening to her, how did she look?" I asked sadly.

"The demons around her were using knives to cut her face and her lips. Her fingers had cuts. The demons would tie her up and cut her. She was screaming in pain. The demons were asking her to dance and when she could not, they would beat and cut her some more."

"Whitney was looking very scary, her hair was shaggy and she wore a tattered black dress that was burning." He described.

"Was she saying anything?"

"She was saying that the people who are listening to her music will go to hell and suffer."

How sad I felt when I heard this terrible news. How I wished I could remove her from hell but it was too late. She had a chance to follow Christ when she was alive on earth. Mnjala was told by Jesus that Whitney's father is in heaven. He was a minister of the Gospel of Jesus and He loved the Lord. Reality struck home again, you and I still have a chance to follow Christ. It is imperative to accept Jesus.

A Walk with Jesus

Wednesday, August 25, 2010, is a day I will never forget. I had taken the boys for a walk in the evening. The two boys had a bicycle and a scooter to play with so they asked me to walk beside them, accompanying them up and down until we were ready to go back to the house. Mungai told me that I should pretend that I have a friend walking with me while he and Mnjala played. I told him that my friend was Jesus.

As soon as I said this, the children exclaimed, "Jesus is here. He is right there next to you!"

"He is waiting for you to walk with Him," added Mungai.

They were pointing at something I could not see, but I knew they could see Jesus. Jesus had visited them many times now, and they had become friends with Him. I simply did not know what to say or do. The King of kings and Lord of lords, the Maker of heaven and earth, was right there next to me, waiting for me to take a walk with Him. I praised Him in my heart.

I really did not deserve this incredible visit by Him. I felt honored and highly favored. There is absolutely no reason why it was me. So we started the special walk, up and down we went. The children kept staring at something.

"What are you looking at?" I asked.

"Jesus, He is shining so brightly," they told me.

Soon after that, the two boys tilted their heads upwards toward the sky, saying they could see Angel Michael and Angel Gabriel and started waving happily up at them.

"They are flying around above us," Mungai said excitedly.

I looked up but could not see the angels. The sky had turned reddish as the sun was setting and darkness was quickly coming. This was all I could see. This is how life is. A lot is going on in the spiritual realm, but we cannot see it.

I said, "Mnjala, I have some prayer requests to present to Jesus."

My little nephew responded, "Jesus has told me that He will be in the computer room after we are done with the walk."

I walked in silence, pondering these things in my heart in great humility.

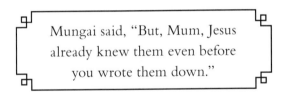

Mungai said, "But, Mum, Jesus already knew them even before you wrote them down."

After I had done ten laps, I announced to the boys that I was going home. As soon as we entered the house, Mnjala ran into the computer room and started talking to Jesus. The little boy looked like he was talking to an empty chair. I went upstairs at the speed of lightning to pick my prayer requests. When I returned, I knelt down and said to the boys, "I am going to read my prayer requests to Jesus."

Mungai said, "But, Mum, Jesus already knew them even before you wrote them down."

Mnjala agreed.

The boys had by now turned to play with some toy cars, just getting on with their lives.

So I said, "I want Jesus to answer what is on the list."

The boys responded, "Jesus has said yes."

Praise the Lord!

A Prophetic Word from Mungai

Just before we had dinner, on the same evening, Mungai called me upstairs and explained to me how Jesus told him He would remind me about my visit to heaven. He said I was fortunate because Jesus Himself would be taking me to heaven while Angel Michael would carry Mnjala and Angel Gabriel would carry him. He also said that he and Mnjala would be taken to hell to fight demons, which he was referring to as ghosts and skeletons.

I asked him, "When would this happen?"

He replied, "It will happen tonight."

This was actually too much for me to take in. I was truly lost in thought. In a few hours, Jesus would take me up with the view of reminding me about my first trip to heaven. Our Lord is definitely full of surprises.

That Very Night

I almost stayed up keeping watch that night, wondering when Jesus would take me to heaven. I even woke up to go to the bathroom at about midnight and then returned to my bed, wondering why I had not yet gone. After a while, I was fast asleep, and then it happened!

In the morning, I told my husband what had transpired that night, and he just remained silent. When the children woke up, they told me that Jesus had carried me while Angel Michael and Angel Gabriel had carried them, as the Lord had revealed the previous evening. I could not remember being in heaven, but I remember the process of getting there. It was a most awesome experience that I will never forget for as long as I live.

This is what happened. I was definitely asleep when a gentle force pushing me from my side of the bed to my husband's side woke me up. My husband was right there next to me, fast asleep. I had absolutely no control of what was taking place. I could not pull myself back to my side of the bed, but I was not afraid. The force moving me was not rough. It was extremely gentle. When I got to the edge of the bed, I was lifted up and out through the window. Then I began going upwards at this incredible speed that I cannot describe in words. I could feel myself because I had all my senses. I knew I had left my body. In fact, at some point, I felt a bit anxious because I pictured myself out there in space all by myself. I could not see Jesus, but right then, He touched me. The moment He touched me, the anxiety left me, and I was at total peace. Instantaneously, I began praising God with every cell in my being. At that very moment, I found myself floating around the stars. They were beautiful and glowing. They looked rounded and not jagged as I would have expected.

A beautiful glow was coming from above, and I thought to myself, *Heaven must be up there, but how will I enter, what will I see, and what will I tell God?*

It felt like I had been there for about five minutes, maybe shorter or longer, I cannot tell. After this, I cannot remember what happened, but I remember going back to my body. It felt like a big thud, and then there I was, awake next to my husband. I thought he had felt something, but later on when I asked him, he said he hadn't felt anything. Now I knew how my son and nephew got to heaven every other time when Jesus came for them. This experience has changed me forever. No matter what my son and nephew say about the supernatural, I believe them. How can I not? It happened to me! God allowed it to happen to me so I can believe.

That same night, Jesus took the children to hell, where they, accompanied by Angel Michael and Angel Gabriel, all fought Satan and his demons. They said they had all sorts of tools in their hands, and they used them to slay, weaken, and destroy these evil creatures. The boys seemed so excited about this experience that they went on and on about it.

Mnjala asked Mungai, "Do you remember that demon who was writing something bad about Jesus on a wall in hell?"

Mungai continued, "Mum, the demon had written that Jesus is bad and He hates people. I snatched the pen from him, and I wrote that Jesus is good and He loves all the people."

This incident teaches us that we who are in Christ are more powerful than Satan and his demons. Jesus has given us power and authority over them. Satan hates us, but God loves us. "You, dear children, are from God and have overcome them, because the one who is in you is greater than the one who is in the world" (1 John 4:4).

Chapter 15

The Ten Commandments

God asked them to read the Ten
Commandments in heaven.

The following day, the children explained to me that I was in the library in heaven reading a golden Bible. God asked them to sit on the golden chairs, and then He showed them the Ten Commandments. The children described the Ten Commandments to be on what appeared like two stone tablets. They said they resembled what they had seen in the Bible books for children. God then asked Mnjala to read the first five commandments and requested Mungai to read the sixth to the tenth one. What an incredible teaching! I was amazed that God was now teaching them about His rules.

The Ten Commandments (Exodus 20)

And God spoke all these words:

1. *You shall have no other gods before me.*

2. *You shall not make for yourself an idol in the form of anything in heaven above or on the earth beneath or in the waters below. You shall not bow down to them or worship them for I the LORD your God, am a jealous God.*

3. *You shall not misuse the name of the LORD your God, for the LORD will not hold anyone guiltless who misuses His name.*

4. *Remember the Sabbath day by keeping it holy. Six days you shall labor and do all your work but the seventh day is a Sabbath to the LORD your God.*

5. *Honor your father and your mother so that you may live long in the land the LORD your God is giving you.*

6. *You shall not murder.*

7. *You shall not commit adultery.*

8. *You shall not steal.*

9. *You shall not give false testimony against your neighbor.*

10. *You shall not covet your neighbor's house. You shall not covet your neighbor's wife, or his manservant or maidservant, his ox or donkey or anything that belongs to your neighbor.*

The fact that God showed these children His commandments means that He expects us to know them and live by them. God also expects parents to teach them to their children, so they, too, may know and follow them.

Many Christians today are compromising their walk with God by breaking His commandments. God expects us to rely on Him so we can live a righteous life. "Remain in me, and I will remain in you. No branch can bear fruit by itself; it must remain in the vine. Neither can you bear fruit unless you remain in me" (John 15:4).

In the New Testament, Jesus summarizes the commandments by saying that the greatest commandment is that we should love the Lord Our God with all our hearts with all our souls and with our minds. And the second is to love your neighbor as yourself, as Matthew 22:34–40 summarizes.

How true is this? If you loved God with your all, would you worship idols? Would you misuse God's name? The answer is no. And if you loved your neighbor as yourself, would you steal from them? Would you give a false testimony against them? Would you have an affair with their wife or husband? The answer again is no.

War in Hell

Then the boys excitedly narrated to me how they went to hell with Jesus, where they fought Satan and his demons again. They described how Jesus made them taller than the trees, which gave them the ability to easily step on these evil creatures. They fought the demons using different weapons that appeared in their hands. Sometimes they had fiery swords like those of the angels, while at other times, they used their fists at other times. They even had the ability to blow them off with a mighty wind. This was seemingly a very exciting experience for both of them because I could hardly get them to calm down.

A Prophetic Word from Mnjala

That evening, we got ready for bed, and then I told the boys that I was going to clip their nails. So while I was in my son's room with Mnjala clipping his nails, he told me that Jesus had just spoken in his heart and told him that He would start appearing to me.

I honestly thought that I had heard wrong, so I asked him, "Can you repeat what you just said?"

He repeated, "Jesus has said that He will start appearing to you."

My heart was overwhelmed when I heard this. I had so many questions. What have I done to deserve this visitation? How does Jesus really look? How will He appear to me? I know that God is always with us and He surrounds us with His presence, but now He wanted to appear to me, that I was going to actually see Him. This is just by His grace, not because of anything I have done. So let it be.

More War in Hell

The boys explained they had visited heaven again, where they had had so much fun playing with kites. Mungai said he picked a kite that had many colors like a rainbow while Mnjala picked a red one. Oh, how I looked forward to flying those kites in heaven. They sounded like so much fun!

After this, Jesus took them back to hell to fight Satan and his demons. Mungai explained to me how Satan kept making more demons so they could hurt God's people. He explained that Satan was using soil and blood to make more creatures and Jesus would ask them to destroy them. They would miraculously find swords in their hands with which they slew the foul creatures. I did not understand everything they said, but I believed them. The children demonstrated and explained that, while they were in hell, Satan would pick soil using his hands, and then he would start forming the shape of a man using it. He would begin with the legs, moving up to the thighs, waist, chest, hands, and finally the head. Other demons would collect blood in bowls from the people in hell, taking it to Satan who would in turn pour it on the bodies he had formed. The blood gave life to these bodies, causing them to rise up and start moving around making horrible noises.

"Wooooo," the boys imitated in an eerie voice.

"They were walking like zombies," Mnjala described them, stretching his hands and walking in zombie-like motion in an attempt to imitate the scary creatures.

Mungai said, "They were so ugly, and their heads were upside down. The eyes were near their necks, and they were red in color."

They recounted how Satan made many of these creatures, which the two boys proceeded to destroy by boxing, throwing, and poking them with their fingers. Satan was surprised that they were easily wiping out his creation.

Mnjala said, "He fell off from his black chair and started running away from us, looking for a place to hide."

They were giggling as they remembered the incident.

Mungai added, "Satan cannot harm us when we have Jesus."

I asked, "How did Satan look?"

Mungai said, "He was half ugly and half beautiful. Mum, remember he was an angel, but he hates everything good that God created."

"You will tread upon the lion and the cobra; you will trample the great lion and the serpent" (Ps. 91:13).

As I pondered over why God would allow the children to see Satan 'creating' demons, I had no way of explaining this event. How could Satan have created creatures in hell? Even when the children shared this event in church, everyone was asking questions. I did not know what to say. The children were simply reporting what they had seen. After all, they had seen much more and the Lord was revealing such incredible things to them in a miraculous manner. I knew that this encounter was going to be a controversial one and I was contemplating removing it all together.

However, one Sunday, many months after this episode, I told the boys that I was going to remove this story from the book. My nephew Mnjala asked Jesus what I should do concerning this part of the book. Then the Lord answered immediately by telling Mnjala in his heart, "Tell her that she did not know that Satan can create demons but now she knows. Tell her to leave the story in the book."

The Bible warns us that we should not be ignorant of the devil's schemes and this story helps to confirm that Satan is always scheming and constantly planning evil. "In order that Satan might not outwit us. For we are not unaware of his schemes" (II Cor. 2:11).

Greeting Jesus

Later that afternoon, I took the boys to a nearby mall to play. We had a lot of fun. After a couple hours, I decided it was getting late, so we left. We entered the car, and I requested the boys to thank Jesus for the nice time we'd had.

"Jesus is right here in the car with us." Mungai said. "He is in the backseat."

"He has now moved to the front seat next to you Mum."

"Well, why don't we greet Jesus?" I suggested. They each extended their hands in turns to greet Him.

"We felt Jesus' hand," they both exclaimed.

I said I wanted to greet Jesus, too. I extended my hand to greet Him, but I did not feel His hand. The children said Jesus had extended His hand to me, too. I was thankful He did. We left and went home to have dinner.

The South Side of Heaven

Mungai woke up excited and explained to me that he and Mnjala had been to heaven at night. He said that God had allowed them to go to the south side of heaven. He described this part of heaven as having a very big and beautiful beach. While there, they swam underwater with the fish. The fish were not scared of them. They could touch them, and then they put them back into the water. Sometimes they would even ride on the big fish like a boat. They also did some fishing, which he described as being so much fun. Mungai said they would even make bubbles underwater by blowing out air through their mouth, sometimes catching a fish inside a big bubble. Then it would free itself, and they would do this over again.

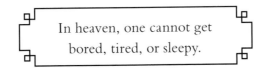

In heaven, one cannot get bored, tired, or sleepy.

There were camels they could ride. These camels would go inside the water while they rode on their backs. Just hearing the excitement in Mungai's voice as he narrated this experience made it sound so enjoyable and amusing to ride on camels underwater.

"In heaven, you are able to do a lot of things that one cannot do here on earth," Mungai enlightened me.

He said, "In heaven, one does not get bored, tired, or sleepy. You can sleep if you want to, but it is not a must. You can sleep as part of enjoying heaven."

They were wearing their favorite colors. Mungai was in a red swimsuit while Mnjala was in a blue one. This made heaven seem like so much more fun. "You have made known to me the path of life you will fill me with joy in your presence, with eternal pleasures at your right hand" (Ps. 16:11).

Mungai thereafter explained that heaven is divided into north, south, east, west, and central. He said that God is in the center of heaven, which is where the throne room is.

"How did you know the directions?"

"I have seen a compass and it has all the directions written on it."

Spiritual Warfare

It was September 18, 2010. Loud noises coming from the top of our roof woke me up in the middle of the night. I sat up because I was actually startled from my sleep and very frightened. My heart was pounding hard and fast. It felt as though it would jump right out of my chest. I felt terror. So I held onto my chest to try to calm myself down. The noises gave me the impression that about thirty thieves were on our rooftop, trying to gain access into our home. I cannot explain why the number thirty came to my mind, but that was the figure I thought of. The banging was extremely loud and disturbing. I wondered where the guard was and why he was not sounding the alarm. What about the neighbors? Surely they could hear this disturbing noise. I wondered how I was going to protect my son because my husband was away. Then something impressed upon my heart that I should pray, and I did exactly that. After I prayed, as suddenly as the loud banging began, it stopped. What was going on? I set off my car alarm so, in case the guard was asleep, the noise would wake him up. But now there was total peace, not a sound, so I went back to sleep.

In the morning, as I was making my bed, I asked Mungai whether he had heard noise from the roof of our house. His response completely shocked me.

He said, "There were demons on top of our roof. Many demons. I think they were more than thirty of them. They had come with hammers, and they were banging on top of our roof. They wanted to damage our roof, and they also wanted to get inside our house."

"What!" I exclaimed in shock and wonder.

"Jesus had made our house strong," he said.

"We had to fight the demons. Mnjala, Angel Michael and Angel Gabriel came to help fight them." Satan had sent the demons. Jesus had come, too, but He was watching as we destroyed the demons. Mum, we destroyed all of them. Then we went to Mnjala's house because demons were at their place, too. We found Jesus there waiting for us. When we finished fighting the demons, we went up to heaven in our toy cars. Jesus made our toy cars big, I had the yellow and red one and Mnjala had the blue and red one. We were moving very fast. We even overtook an airplane. When we got to heaven, our toy cars became gold in color, and we left the cars outside the throne room. We sat on the golden chair.

God told us, "The cars are very nice."

He then gave Mungai a promise, which I do not feel at liberty to reveal at this time.

Later that day, Mungai had more to explain. He said, "Mum, at night a demon had picked your best dress from the wardrobe and tried to tear it but I kicked the demon and he went through the wall and back to hell. Mum, this happened right before you woke up to pray because I saw you. I also saw our satellite dish is white in color. I saw it while we were on the roof fighting off the demons."

Mungai has previously never seen our satellite dish. That is why this and the fact that he reported having seen me waking up to pray were solid confirmations that he did actually see and participate in events of that night.

"Mum, demons hate both God and people and that is why they were attacking our homes." Mungai concluded.

War with Satan and His Demons

On the morning of September 26, 2010, I asked Mungai if they had gone to heaven. He told me that they had, but they had spent most of the night fighting Satan. He said Satan had come and told them that he had come to kill them and he would start with Mungai because he was the older one. Mungai said demons had also been sent from hell, and they were so many that they covered the neighbors' roofs. There are ten maisonettes on our compound so I cannot imagine how many demons would cover them, but they surely must have been many. Angel Michael, Angel Gabriel, and Mnjala were in the fight, too, while Jesus was watching them from heaven. Mungai explained to me that they kicked and boxed the demons and would smite them using fiery swords. They fought and defeated Satan and his demons!

Mungai also told me that a demon wanted to hurt me while I slept. It wanted to pull my legs. He again pushed that demon back to hell. Yes, Jesus has given us authority to trample over Satan and his demons. The children had the opportunity to literally do this. They now have total confidence in God that they can defeat the enemy. "You, dear children, are from God and have overcome them, because the one who is in you is greater than the one who is in the world" (1 John 4:4).

On that Saturday morning, Mungai said, "Mum, I saw you in heaven. You were singing and playing an instrument to God. The instrument was made out of gold and you held one on each hand and banged them together making a beautiful sound to God." From his description, the instrument sounded like a cymbal. I was in total amazement. I am a visual person and so I asked, "What was I wearing?"

"You wore your red pajamas but the pink flowers on the pajamas were shining like gold."

"God had asked me and Mnjala to look at you through a window." Mungai said as he ran off to get a toy.

War with Satan

On October 30, 2010, the boys fought head-on with the devil. As we were driving to church Mungai reported, "Mnjala and I fought with Satan at night."

"What?"

"Jesus came and picked me up from my bed and took me to hell where we fought Satan." We fought from somewhere above hell because we could see people burning below us."

"Satan had come armed because he was afraid of us." Mungai chuckled. "He was wearing a special suit. It was black in color with red strips and fitting everywhere. This outfit had something on the chest. It was two crossed bones and an ugly head with red eyes."

Mungai explained that Satan threatened that he would defeat them because of the outfit he was wearing. He also had a helmet on his head. The children were in their pajamas, nothing special. Jesus was watching them from heaven as they fought Satan. This time round, Angel Michael and Angel Gabriel did not come down to help them either. They were also watching with Jesus from heaven.

> *In addition to all this, take up the shield*
> *of faith, with which you can extinguish*
> *all the flaming arrows of the evil one.*
> *Ephesians 6:16*

Satan started shooting fiery bullets at the children, but they could not be harmed. An invisible shield seemed to be around them. As the fiery bullets were coming out of Satan's hands, they would bounce off and not come anywhere close to them. Satan continued to throw some more. At first, he was shooting a few, and then he increased them by number and speed. He made them come faster and faster, but they would not go through the shield. They fought him back. Mnjala took the lead. Satan had told them that he was going to kill them and he would start with Mnjala this time round. Mnjala used his fists to box him and his feet to kick him. Mungai asked Mnjala if he could allow him to finish the battle.

Mungai, amazed by the power and authority Jesus had accorded them, said, "Mum, I barely kicked Satan with my foot, and he fell down into hell below us. He was screaming the whole time. He landed with a loud thud, and stones and rocks scattered around where he had fallen."

The boys defeated Satan! Halleluiah! We are more than conquerors in Christ Jesus.

The Bible has warned us that we are in constant battle with Satan and his demons. The Bible says the battle is not against flesh and blood but against rulers, authorities, powers of this dark world, and evil spirits in the heavenly realms. We are taught to put on the full armor of God so we can take a stand against the evil one.

> Stand firm then, with the belt of truth buckled around your waist, with the breastplate of righteousness in place, and with your feet fitted with the readiness that comes from the gospel of peace. In addition to all this, take up the shield of faith, with which you can extinguish all the flaming arrows of the evil one. Take the helmet of salvation and the sword of the Spirit, which is the word of God (Eph. 6:14–17).

What stood out for me in this story is the fact that Satan was throwing fiery arrows at the children while they had a shield of protection around them. The children's account is just as the

Bible reports. We are warned that Satan attacks using flaming or fiery arrows as the children saw, and we are admonished to arm ourselves with God's armor. The children had an invisible shield around them, which stopped Satan's darts. The shield, as the Scripture above describes, is faith. Indeed, the boys have learned to trust in Jesus. They had faith that Jesus would watch over them while at war with the devil, and that is why they overcame him.

After winning the fight, the children went up to heaven. I must add that they thrashed Satan thoroughly. He had no chance of overpowering them, yet they are children. They are children who belong to God. So are you and I.

Mums in Heaven and Hell

One of the most difficult parts to understand in all these experiences is why God would take the children's parents to heaven and hell and remove the memory of it all from them? But I know that God has answers to everything, and it is just a matter of time before the Holy Spirit reveals all this to us.

It was after school and I was having this conversation with Mungai.

"Mum, you and Mnjala's mum are going to heaven and hell tonight."

I was so stunned. I asked him, "Who has told you this?"

He simply replied, "Mum, you know who has told me, here in my heart."

"The mums will go to heaven and hell on Friday night and the dads will go on Saturday night." He added.

"What!" I was puzzled and a bit anxious because I knew for certain that Jesus had spoken to Mungai.

I felt anxious because I did not want to visit hell. From what I had heard from the children and what I had read, hell is not the best of places to visit.

For this reason, I asked Mungai, "Tell Jesus that I do not want to visit hell. Tell Him that I already believe that hell is a real place."

Mungai answered, "Jesus has already said. He never changes His mind."

The following morning, I woke up filled with praises in my heart. I told Mungai that I could not remember being in heaven, but he told me he would give me the details later. At this point in our lives, I had learned to be patient with my little boy. Sometimes he would tell me things later because he did not feel like talking about them then. I respected that.

Later that morning, he told me that my sister Janet and I had been in heaven singing to God. He said we were dressed in robes that looked like Joseph's coat. "They had many colors like the rainbow. You sang many of the songs we sing in church."

He said that we also went to hell after we had finished with heaven. Jesus had asked the two boys to each hold the hands of their mothers, and then down to hell we descended. While in hell, as Mungai described to me, we watched Satan's demons worshipping him.

Dads in Heaven and Hell

That evening, Mungai told me that the dads would go to heaven first and thereafter to hell. He said I would see his dad in my dream, which would be the sign to prove to me his dad had gone to the two places. On August 28, 2010, God had told Mnjala that this was going to happen.

He told him, "I can see that your dads do not believe. I am going to take them to heaven and hell on October 9, 2010."

I woke up the next morning, very anxious to know whether the dads had gone to heaven and hell. I remembered seeing Mungai's dad in my dream. It was the strangest thing that has ever happened to me. First of all, I felt transfixed to my bed, and then I saw this thing that looked like a figure of a man approaching me. It was weird. I cannot even describe it. But as this figure came close to me, it became a person. It was Waiyaki, my husband. I could see him very clearly. He was standing right in front of me wearing a blue and yellow polo shirt that I had bought him. Then in what seemed like just a few seconds, the dream was over. Indeed, just as Mungai had told me, I saw his dad in my dream. I knew that God had visited.

> Mungai explained that, in heaven, his dad was wearing the colored robe like Joseph's coat and Mnjala's dad was in a white robe that had a golden sash around the waist.

So I proceeded to ask Mungai, "Had the dads been to heaven and hell?"

He simply responded, "Yes."

He did not provide the details then, but he said he would explain later. We later spoke on the phone with Waiyaki, who was away at the time, and I told him what our son had said about him being in heaven and hell that night. He sounded very surprised, but just like me, he had no recollection of the experience.

That Sunday morning, Mnjala, his mum, and sisters came to our house so we could go to church together. It was a grand opportunity for the two boys to relate their dads' experience to us. It was just amazing watching them talk and finish each other's sentences. Obviously, they had been together that night. Mungai explained that, while in heaven, his dad was wearing a colored robe like Joseph's coat while Mnjala's dad wore a white robe with a golden sash around the waist. He said that Our Lord Jesus spoke to their dads.

Jesus told them, "I have been taking your sons to heaven and to hell.

The dads replied, "We believe."

Next, Jesus instructed each child to hold his own father's hand, and down they descended into hell. Mungai said the fathers were very fearful. He explained that Mnjala's dad was running around helter-skelter crying out loudly, "Please somebody get me out of this place," while his own dad was shouting, "Mungai, please do not leave my hand." At that juncture, Mungai pointed out Jesus to his father, telling him that He was present so he needn't be afraid.

The boys laughed at the fact that their dads were so scared of hell. Mungai said that two demons came for his father, and he pushed them away from him. His father stepped on them hard, and they were destroyed. They destroyed many more demons together with his father. The same thing happened to Mbugua, Mnjala's daddy. As he was screaming and running around, he stepped on several demons, destroying them instantly. The kids narrated that they were in the part of hell where there were cages. This same part also had some pits in which some people were burning and hopping up and down, crying for help. My sister and I were so amazed to hear them talk about their daddies in this way. I pray that the two dads will remember their experience, but nevertheless, I know God planted something in their spirits. It appears that God wants to use them, too.

Sometime in the month of December, my sister Janet and Mnjala came over to visit us. As we were just catching up with my sister, the two boys came to play around us.

"Mnjala informed us saying, "Jesus has told me that my dad can remember a part of his experience in hell. He remembers screaming and running around hopelessly."

I exclaimed in excitement, "What?"

Mnjala said, "Jesus said that my dad is afraid to say that he was taken to hell."

My sister then said, "I have noticed for some time he was afraid to go to bed. There is a specific night when he was screaming in his sleep. It could be the day he remembered because I have never heard him yell in his sleep. I woke him up and asked him what the problem was, and he refused to answer."

I am certain that God wants to help the boys' fathers to live for Him so that they in turn will help others in the future. They now believe Our Lord Jesus visited their sons and have shown them heaven and hell.

Chapter 16

God Feeds the Boys Honey in Heaven

On October 18, 2010, I was just about to tuck Mungai into bed when he started to tell me about heaven. He said he and Mnjala had been to heaven the previous night. As they were in heaven playing and surfing on water, they heard God's big voice calling them.

He explained to me that God's voice was so big that the whole of heaven heard Him. "God's voice can even make someone deaf, and the light that comes from Him is so bright that it can make someone blind."

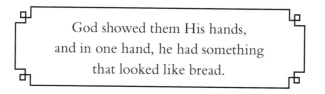

God showed them His hands, and in one hand, he had something that looked like bread.

Then he said that, when God called them, they went to the throne room at great speed and found their golden chairs waiting for them.

"God has written our names on the chairs, our three names," he added.

They sat down, each on his chair. Mungai said that God showed them His hands, and in on one hand, He had something that looked like bread. He told the children that this was manna. Then He went ahead to rub it in His hand, and within a few seconds, the manna became honey. God poured the honey into one bottle, the bottle became two bottles, and He gave one bottle to Mungai and the other to Mnjala. He asked them to eat the honey. Wow!

This story totally baffled me. I realized that, at the time, the boys had been going to heaven every single day for almost two weeks. I remembered that, on their first visit to heaven, they had sat on one golden chair together. On another visit, the chair had split into two. This time round, God had made two chairs for them, one chair for each boy with their individual names on each chair.

The fact that God fed them with honey during this particular visit is also very significant. Honey in the Bible signifies the word of God. I remember a song we used to sing in Sunday school many years ago. "God's word is so sweet; it is sweeter than honey and the honeycomb." In the Old Testament, God gave the prophet Ezekiel a scroll, and he was asked to eat it. The scroll contained the word of God, and it tasted like honey.

Then I looked, and I saw a hand stretched out to me. In it was a scroll which he unrolled before me. On both sides of it were written words of lament and mourning and woe. And he said to me, "Son of man, eat what is before you, eat this scroll then go and speak to the house of Israel. So I opened my mouth and he gave me the scroll to eat. Then he said to me, "Son of man eat this scroll I am giving you and fill your stomach with it'. So I ate it and it tasted as sweet as honey in my mouth (Ezek. 2:9–3:3).

Fear in Hell

One night, Mungai woke up in the middle of the night and asked me to pray for him. He said he had a bad dream in which he saw many people being thrown into a very deep hole. The people were very scared. Satan and his demons had a machine that they were using to suck up the brains of these people. Mungai was literally shaking as he held me tightly close. He was very afraid. I had never seen him so scared. I prayed for him, and he thankfully went back to sleep.

The following day after school, Mungai explained to me that he had been in hell together with Jesus and Mnjala. He told me that Mnjala was afraid as well. I noted this was the first time the Lord had allowed them to feel the fear in hell. It occurred to me that, on previous visits, Our Lord Jesus had been protecting them from experiencing the fear that the people in hell feel. The children had never expressed that they felt afraid in hell. They were usually observers with Jesus always by their side or watching them from heaven.

In *23 Minutes in Hell*, Bill Wiese describes the fear he felt in hell. Jesus had also shown him hell, but he was allowed to experience the torment in hell. Though he is a Christian, he was sent to hell as an unbeliever and left there by Jesus. He experienced the emotions unbelievers feel in hell. Indescribable fear gripped him when twelve-foot-tall demons came to torment him. He could not bear the darkness, pain, loneliness, and heart-wrenching cries of those in hell. He felt the fire in hell, the hopelessness, and, worse still, the torment by demons. But even after the Lord brought him back to his body, he was still so horrified that his wife had to pray fervently for him.

One day, Mungai told me how he saw worms eating people in hell. He had also seen rats and snakes crawling everywhere in hell. "There are many many worms in hell. The worms do not get burned away in the fire, and the more someone tries to remove them, the more they come."

What a dreadful place to be, I thought.

"And they will go out and look upon the dead bodies of those who rebelled against me; their worm will not die, nor will their fire be quenched, and they will be loathsome to all mankind" (Isa. 66:24).

Hell is definitely a place you do not want to go to. It has all the negative emotions like fear, sadness, loneliness, regret, self-pity, hatred, and hopelessness. Please ensure that you do not go there!

The Journey Alone to Heaven

On one of the weeks, God had told them that they could go to heaven on their own any time during the night as it pleased them. He said they were to continue going in this way until the time God decided they should stop.

So Mungai told me that he would go out floating through the window or the roof. Then he would meet with his cousin at the planets, and they would go upwards together until they reached heaven, where they would enter through a window. He told me they would pass the planets every time they were going up and even as they were coming down. Their descent back to earth was pretty amazing. They would sometimes just float back, or at times, the Lord would give them parachutes of various descriptions. Sometimes, the parachutes would have many colors; other times, they would be golden in color. Mungai explained that sometimes the parachutes had their pictures on them, and occasionally, each boy would be given a parachute with their favorite color or their names written on them. But these parachutes, whatever their description, would be shining so much because of the light from the sun as they floated downward through the planets and back home.

"Mum, the parachutes were so beautiful. They were shining like diamonds," Mungai explained to me.

During that period, Mungai told me that, as he was leaving the house, sometimes he would look at the time, and he noticed it was ten minutes to eleven. On another occasion, he looked at the time again, and he noted that it was midnight.

I wondered whether they were scared on their way to heaven, but Mungai reassured me that they were not afraid of anything because God was always watching over them from heaven and He made sure they got there safely. He also excitedly said that they saw all the planets. He informed me what was around Saturn. We all know from science that it has a ring around it.

Mungai had information about this ring. "Planet Saturn has small moons and rocks that make the ring around it. It is a very rich planet. I see small gold rings around it. Like the ones you are wearing on your fingers."

I was at a loss for words.

Thanking God

Just before we went to bed on October 28, 2010, I asked Mungai to tell God a big "Thank you." I wanted him to tell God trillion, million thanks because He has done such great things in our lives.

I told Mungai, "You have been asking God for so many things throughout the week, so tonight you should just go and tell God thanks."

He added that, because the following day was his birthday, he would ask God for good weather. He did not want it to be raining while he cut his birthday cake at school. We had agreed that I would take cake and some sweets to his school so he could celebrate his birthday with his classmates.

The following day, Mungai woke up excited because it was his birthday. It was Mnjala's birthday, too, because, as I mentioned earlier, the two boys were born on the same date but a year apart. His dad and I wished him a happy birthday, and we left for school.

A Birthday Party in Heaven

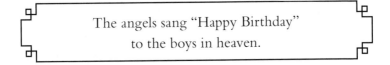

The angels sang "Happy Birthday"
to the boys in heaven.

On the way to school, Mungai reported that God had wished them a happy birthday in heaven.

I exclaimed, "What?"

He said that, while in heaven, they each sat on their golden chair in front of God, and God told them in His big voice, "Mungai and Mnjala, happy birthday!"

Then I inquired a little more concerning this story, and Mungai explained that the angels prepared two cakes, a square one for him and a round one for Mnjala. They decorated the throne room. They decorated it with beautifully colored balloons in orange, green, yellow, blue, white, and red. Then God cut the cakes, and the angels helped serve them as they sang *'Happy Birthday'* to the two boys. Everyone including Jesus was there with them. They ate the cakes and celebrated. Others present at the party were the disciples of Jesus, John the Baptist, Moses, David, Abraham, Sarah, Joseph and his brothers, Samuel, Joseph, and Mary. Uncle Ken was also present for the birthday. Oh my! I was totally bewildered.

Mungai added, "Everyone celebrates his birthday in heaven, even Moses, Abraham, Joseph, and others."

God obviously knows when each one of us was born, including the Old Testament folk.

My son said gleefully, "Oh, Mum, the cakes were very yummy, like black forest but better."

"Ah!" I said in total astonishment.

"Did you remember to give thanks to God?"

"Yes, I did. God said okay."

God also told the children the weather would be good on that day, and it was. The sun shone brightly in a clear blue sky, with no signs of the cold, drizzly days we had been experiencing. What a mighty God we serve!

The False Gods

During the Diwali weekend in October, Mungai and I went to a shopping mall in Nairobi's Westlands area. Diwali is a festival that is popularly known as the Festival of Lights. Believers of the Hindu and Jain faith celebrate it between mid-October and mid-November. During Diwali, there is the lighting of small clay lamps filled with oil to signify the triumph of good over evil. The adherents wear new clothes, light fireworks, and share sweets and other snacks with family and friends.

So when we got to the mall, we found a section of the mall had been designated for the selling of Hindu gods. These gods had been beautifully displayed with lights around them as the Diwali festivities were underway. We walked around, just staring at them. Indeed, they are just something to behold. Some have very big bellies while others look part elephant and part human. There were so many of them and in different shapes, colors, and sizes. I explained to Mungai that Hindus worship these statues.

As we were going into the supermarket, Mungai stopped me and whispered in my ear, "Mum, I want to tell you something."

"What is it, son?"

"I saw many demons in those gods that we were looking at. Each one of those gods had demons inside it. The demons had black bodies and red eyes. They knew I could see them, and they told me they were coming for me tonight."

"Oh my God! Let me pray for you right now," I pleaded with him.

But he dismissed me. "Mum, it is okay. I'm not afraid. God told me in my heart not to be afraid, so I am not. Do not worry, Mum."

> "Mum, I can see a demon inside the place where the Indian lady is. This demon does not even have legs. The place where there should be legs, I can see something like a tail."

When we left the supermarket, we saw an Indian woman lighting candles in a small area that she had set apart for herself. Several other women had brought their small girls aged between eight and ten years. These girls were being asked to remove their shoes and step into the area with candles. I was wondering what ritual was being performed and what impact it would have on the girls' lives.

Then I noticed that Mungai was staring intently toward all this activity.

"What's wrong?" I asked him.

"Mum, I can see a demon inside the area where the Indian lady is. This demon does not even have legs. The place where there should be legs, I can see something like a tail. It looks like a ghost."

All this surprised me a great deal. This was the first time Mungai could see demons during the day, which meant that God had allowed him to see into the supernatural.

As we left, Mungai told me he was concerned about the people who were worshipping idols because they would not make it to heaven. He wondered why anyone would worship something made by hand and can break after falling down. He said God in heaven would ask them why they worshipped idols instead of the true God. Mungai continued to tell me that, when everyone dies, whether they were good or bad people, they will have to face God first. I was amazed at the great insight my son was showing concerning the things of God. "Just as man is destined to die once, and after that to face judgment" (Heb. 9:27).

When we got home later that day, my son told me that he could see many demons in some of our neighbors' homes. He singled out the homes with the statues similar to the ones that we had seen earlier in the shopping mall.

In the Ten Commandments, God commands us not to worship idols. He wants us to worship Him alone because He is the one and only true God. He is God, the king of this universe. He made us so we can worship Him and Him alone.

About Idols

In the Bible, God proves Himself to be the only true God in so many ways. The story of prophet Elijah is recorded in the book of Kings, where the prophet summons all Israel and the prophets of Baal to a contest on Mount Carmel to see who the true God is. The duel involved Prophet Elijah on one hand and the prophets of Baal on the other. Each of them was to cry out to their god, and the god who answered by burning up the sacrifice by fire was to prove himself as the true God. The prophets of Baal prepared their sacrifice on the altar and spent the day praying to Baal, but nothing happened. Then Elijah set up his sacrifice on the altar and even had water poured three times around the altar, on the wood, and on the sacrifice. As soon as Elijah called on the everlasting God, fire came down and consumed the sacrifice, the wood, the stones, and the earth and even dried up the water! After this, all the people believed and bowed down to worship the true God of heaven.

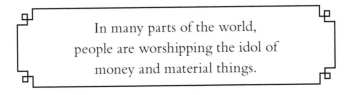

In many parts of the world, people are worshipping the idol of money and material things.

In the olden days, people would carve gods out of wood and stone, and they would worship these carvings. These are false gods because they have simply been made by man's hands. Today, in different parts of the world, people still make gods and worship them just like the ones my son and I saw at the shopping mall. The Bible warns us against these carved images.

"All who make idols are nothing, and the things they treasure are worthless. Those who would speak up for them are blind; they are ignorant, to their own shame. Who shapes a god and casts an idol which can profit him nothing?" (Isa. 44:9–10).

Half of the wood he burns in the fire; over it he prepares his meal, he roasts his meat and eats his fill. He also warms himself and says, Ah! I am warm; I see the fire. From the rest he makes a god, his idol; he bows down to it and worships. He prays to it and says, "Save me; you are my god." They know nothing, they understand nothing; their eyes are plastered over so they cannot see, and their minds closed so they cannot understand. No one stops to think, no one has the knowledge or understanding to say, "Half of it I used for fuel; I even baked bread over its coals, I roasted meat and I ate. Shall I make a detestable thing from what is left? Shall I bow down to a block of wood?" (Isa. 44:16–19).

In *A Divine Revelation of Hell*, Mary K. Baxter writes about a woman she saw in hell who worshipped idols while alive here on earth.

We walked on to another cell. A woman sat picking worms off her bones. She began to cry when she saw Jesus. "Help me Lord," she said. "I will be good. Please let me out." She arose and clenched the bars of the cell. I felt such great pity for her. As she cried, sobs shook her body. She said, "Lord, when I was on earth, I worshipped the Hindu gods and many idols. I would not believe the Gospel the missionaries preached to me, although I heard it many times. One day I died. I cried for my gods to save me from hell, but they could not. Now Lord, I would like to repent." "It's too late," said Jesus.[8]

Idols are, however, not just in the form of handmade gods. An idol is anything that one allows to take first place in his or her life instead of God. In many parts of the world, people are worshipping the idol of money and material things. Many of us are busy looking for more money, more property, more business ventures, more cars, and more and more of all sorts of things,

---

8   Baxter, *A Divine Revelation of Hell*, 1993.

and we have forgotten God. Among us, there are also those who are worshipping idols of power, false religion, the flesh, and witchcraft. Many are investing a lot of their money, time, and energy in the pursuit of these gods and have turned away from the true God, the only one who can fill the emptiness in our lives. We have loved other things more than Him. If you have been praying to an object or through an object, that practice is called idolatry, and God is not pleased with it.

I have written this book to help you realize that there is a God who lives in heaven who loves you and wants you to worship Him alone. If you love your car, house, spouse, children, clothes, a celebrity, or anything else more than God, it is an idol in your life, and you need to bring it down. Anything that takes up more of your attention than God is an idol. In God's Word, He has commanded us to put Him first with no other god before Him. God expects us to give Him our full attention. He is worth it. Idol worshipping leads to hell.

Chapter 17

Mnjala's Mum Healed

In the beginning of the month of November 2010, Mnjala's mum had been suffering a lot of pain on her left leg. The pain was around the ankle and had been going on for almost two weeks. She was wondering what the cause of the problem was and whether she needed to see a doctor.

As she was about to leave for work one Monday morning, she asked Mnjala to pray for her leg. After he prayed, Mnjala told her that Jesus spoke to him and told him that his mother should put her leg in the swimming pool once she got to work.

He told her, "Jesus says he has healed many people with water, like the blind man in the Bible who He had made mud and asked him to go and wash in the pool. Also Naaman who had leprosy was healed in water. He was asked to bathe in the pool seven times, and the leprosy was gone. Jesus wants to heal you with water also."

His answer quite surprised her, but she was convinced that her son had heard from Jesus. When she got to work, she did not immediately go to the pool but tried to work, dragging along her painful leg. When the pain became too unbearable and feeling she had nothing to lose anyway, she went and dunked her throbbing leg into the pool. The healing was immediate. The ailing leg stopped paining. She tells me that the leg that got healed has become much stronger than the other one.

The same Jesus who healed people over two thousand years ago can heal you today. He never changes. He is the same yesterday, today, and forever more.

> Jesus went throughout Galilee teaching in their synagogues, preaching the good news of the kingdom and healing every disease and sickness among the people. News about Him spread all over Syria and people brought to Him all who were ill with various disease, those suffering severe pain, the demon-possessed, those having seizures and the paralyzed, and he healed them (Matt. 4:23–25).

In *We Saw Heaven*, Roberts Liardon recounts how he was shown storehouses in heaven during his visit there when he was eight years old. In one of these storehouses, he saw exterior parts of the human body, all different colors, corresponding to different ethnic groups. "This building contained all the parts of the human body that people on earth need, but Christians have not realized these blessings are waiting for them in Heaven. There is no place else in the universe for these parts to go except right here on earth; no one else needs them."[9]

If you are sick today, ask Jesus to heal you. He is the one who made us, so He can also fix whatever is bothering our bodies. The doors of the storehouse are never locked, but they are always open for those who need to go in. Praise God for this!

---

9   Liardon, *We Saw Heaven*, 2000.

The Hem of Jesus' Garment

So Jesus went with him. A large crowd followed and pressed around Him. And a woman was there who had been subject to bleeding for twelve years. She had suffered a great deal under the care of many doctors and had spent all she had, yet instead of getting better she grew worse. When she heard about Jesus, she came up behind Him in the crowd and touched His cloak because she thought, "If I just touch His clothes, I will be healed." Immediately her bleeding stopped and she felt in her body that she was freed from her suffering. At once Jesus realized that power had gone out from Him. He turned around in the crowd and asked, "Who touched my clothes?" "You see the people crowding against you," His disciples answered and yet you can ask, 'Who touched Me?'" But Jesus kept looking around to see who had done it. Then the woman knowing what had happened to her came and fell at His feet and trembling with fear told Him the whole truth. He said to her, "Daughter, your faith has healed you. Go in peace and be freed from your suffering" (Mark 5:24–34).

Now what you have just read is an incredible story from the Bible of a woman who had suffered for many years with an incurable disease. Doctor upon doctor had tried to help her but without success. When she encountered Jesus, she knew in her heart that, if she touched Him, she would be set free from her infirmity. I can picture this woman crawling on all fours to reach the hem of Jesus' garment. People must have stepped on her as she struggled to weave through the thronging crowd that had gathered around the Lord.

We can all identify with this woman because each one of us has suffered some kind of affliction in our lives. From this story, we learn that Jesus can end our afflictions. He has time for each of us, and we are all very important to Him. Jesus not only healed the woman, but He also told her to go in peace. He healed both her body and her mind. That is the work of our God. Perfect peace and healing comes from Him.

> I could not get over this thought, *Jesus had showed me the hem of His garment!*

One early morning in December 2010, I felt an incredible power come over me. I was asleep, but this immense power that made me feel completely helpless surrounded me. Then I saw this brilliant light that looked like a robe or garment, but I could only see its hem. It was extremely brilliant, almost blinding, but the sight of it did not disturb me. I felt such an overwhelming peace, love, and joy as I gazed at this beautiful sight. Before long, I heard a voice in my heart telling me that I was looking at the hem of Jesus' garment.

I was amazed. I could not get over this thought, *Jesus had showed me the hem of His garment!*

It was difficult to believe that I had actually seen the hem of the Lord's robe. After I woke up from this vision, amazement filled me. I knew the Lord had come to give me His peace and healing, just like He did for the woman in the Bible.

In Mark 6:15, we read that many people touched the edge of the cloak of Jesus and were healed. "And wherever he went—into villages, towns or countryside—they placed the sick in the marketplaces. They begged Him to let them touch even the edge of His cloak and all who touched Him were healed."

I want to encourage you to focus on Jesus and allow Him to come and heal you. Whatever you may be going through—heartache, physical pain, financial difficulties, a broken marriage, a sick child, death of a loved one, loss of a job, or broken family relationships—Jesus is able to bring it to pass.

Another Test

On November 6, 2010, we were celebrating Mungai and Mnjala's birthday at their favorite venue, the Village Market. The boys and their friends love this place because they love to swim and ride on the water slides all day long. Remember, I had taken cake and sweets to Mungai's school on October 29, 2010, and the weather had been great.

Well, when we woke up on the morning of November 6, 2010, at about 6:00 a.m., it was raining heavily. I immediately started wondering how we were going to have an outdoor party in this rain. Mungai had mentioned to his dad and me that God would make the weather nice so we could have fun. I decided to ask Mungai if he knew anything about the weather. I felt rather silly posing that kind of question to a little boy. He told me that God had spoken in his heart and said the weather would change.

After about two hours, it was still raining so I called my sister, Mnjala's mother, who was already at the Village Market to find out what the weather was like on that side of the city. To my dismay, she told me that it was raining so heavily that the tents could not be erected ready for the party because the workers could not go out to do the work. I wondered if my son had heard God right, so I asked him again whether the sun would come out.

He said, "Yes, Mum. God has told me to tell you that you will even see blue in the sky, and we will have a wonderful birthday party. You're too warmly dressed for the day. Remove some of the clothing you are wearing because you would get too hot and uncomfortable."

I stared at him and then out through the window. It looked hopelessly cold and grey.

I thought to myself, *I'm not going to change the venue of the party, but I will believe the word of God.*

I remembered the many times that God had come through for us. In situations that looked so grim, Jesus would suddenly bring a touch from heaven and rescue the situation.

At about midday, my sister Janet called me. "I don't know what has happened here. The weather has suddenly changed, and the sun is out."

You cannot imagine my excitement on hearing this. We went out and had a fabulous time. My son later told me that he saw Jesus at the birthday party. God was teaching us to trust in Him through all situations.

The Lamb's Book of Life

One day as we were going about our daily routine, Mungai started to tell me about a big book he has seen in heaven. "This book is so big and it has names of people written in alphabetical order." He added that the angels wrote the names in this book and they would return from earth every day to add more names into it.

"These are names of the people who will go to heaven because they believe in Jesus," Mungai informed me.

I knew about this book, but it was so refreshing to hear it from my little son. The Bible mentions this book. "Nothing impure will ever enter it, nor will anyone who does what is shameful or deceitful, but only those whose names are written in the Lamb's book of life" (Rev. 21:27). "However, do not rejoice that the spirits submit to you, but rejoice that your names are written in heaven" (Luke 10:20).

Fruits in Heaven

One afternoon during a visit to my mother together with Mnjala and Mungai, she brought out a bowl of fruits for us to have after lunch. At that point, Mnjala informed us that they had eaten fruits in heaven the previous night.

Mungai joined in the conversation. "The fruits in heaven are so sweet that, when you eat them, the juices drip all over you but without getting you dirty."

Later that evening during dinner, Mungai picked up the story about the fruits in heaven. He first and foremost said that, when God sends you for something in heaven, you have to go very fast. This could indicate that God demands obedience from us. Anyway, I asked him what he meant.

He replied, "God sent me to bring an orange, an apple and a glass of water." Mnjala joined in to say, "God asked me to bring grapes, a pineapple and sugarcane."

The children reported that they picked these fruits from a garden in heaven and then took them to God in the throne room.

"Mum, God removed His big hand from the light that covers Him, and He shared the fruit with us. We did not see His face because it shines too much, but we knew He was eating the fruit."

Mungai said, "God does not need to eat, but He wanted to share the fruit with us."

"The sugarcane was so sweet. Today when we go back to heaven, I want to eat it again." Mnjala concluded.

The children have eaten fruits several times in heaven since that first time. They have also reported how they have eaten all kinds of food in heaven that tastes much sweeter than the food we eat here on earth. Whenever they have talked about a celebration in heaven, they also mention that there was food to be eaten. I have therefore come to learn that there is indeed food in heaven. The Bible talks of one particular occasion, the wedding supper of the Lamb prepared for all God's children. This supper will take place after the Rapture, and it will be a celebration in heaven between the bride that is the church and Jesus Christ, who is the groom. This means there will be food for this celebration in heaven. There is no celebration without food!

Christians refer to the Rapture as "being caught up," described in the biblical passage of 1 Thessalonians 4:17, that is, when those who have died believing in Christ and those who are still alive but believe in Christ will be caught up in the clouds to meet the Lord Jesus.

> For the Lord Himself will come down from heaven, with a loud command, with a voice of an archangel, and with the trumpet call of God and the dead in Christ will rise first. After that, we who are still alive and are left will be caught up together with them in the clouds to meet the Lord in the air. And so we be with the Lord forever (1 Thess. 4:16–17).

"Then the angel said to me, 'Write: Blessed are those who are invited to the wedding supper of the Lamb!' And he added, 'These are the true words of God'" (Rev. 19:9).

Jesus and Angels at a Church Service

The Lord confirmed again on this beautiful Sunday morning that His Word is indeed true and should be followed. We were seated at our usual spot in church when Mnjala reported casually that he could see Jesus at the front of the church. He went ahead to point at where Jesus was standing. Mungai backed him up by saying that he could also see Jesus, who Angel Michael and Angel Gabriel accompanied. He said that Angel Gabriel seemed to be busy writing something on a piece of paper. I was curious to know what the angel was recording. Mnjala said he was writing what was going on in the service, noting down whether people were paying attention or not.

After the praise and worship session, I told our pastor that the children had seen Jesus in the service. The pastor led us into more worship, now with the full realization that Jesus was present in our midst.

I thought about Jesus being in every service around the world every single day of the week. Jesus shows up in every place where He is exalted. "For where two or three gather in my name, there am I with them" (Matt. 18:20).

After the church service, we went and sat at a restaurant just next to our church premises. We ordered lunch and chatted with the children as we waited to be served. After a while, Pastor George came and joined us at our table. He wanted to ask the boys what they had seen during the church service. Before long, the two boys told him that Jesus was still right there with us and the two mighty archangels still accompanied Him. The pastor wanted to know exactly where Jesus was.

Mnjala stood up and pointed. "He is right here behind you. Michael is behind my seat, and Gabriel is behind Mungai's seat."

Each time I heard that Jesus the King was in our midst, I felt overwhelmed. I wanted to cry and laugh at the same time. I wished I could reach out and touch Him. I urged Pastor George to hug Jesus because he knew where He was standing. So he stood up and embraced Jesus.

He looked like he was hugging the air, but the children exclaimed in excitement, "Jesus is hugging you, Pastor George." He sat down, and I could tell from the look on his face that he had sensed the Lord's touch.

Then he asked the children, "Is Jesus saying anything?"

Mnjala answered, "He has said that you will live a long life on earth if you continue to preach His word."

These were profound words. I am almost certain that it was another confirmation for our pastor that he had indeed heard God's calling to be a shepherd of His flock. I was praising God in my heart. Then almost in unison, the boys advised the pastor that Jesus said He would take care of his money and He would make sure that it does not run out. I praised God even more because it confirmed that He is involved in every area of our lives, including our finances.

Go to Church!

"Let us not give up meeting together, as some are in the habit of doing, but let us encourage one another and all the more as you see the Day approaching" (Heb. 10:25). The word of God has commanded us to meet, gather, and fellowship together. There is a lot to draw from meeting with other believers. The apostle Paul in the New Testament compares each member of the church to the different parts of a body. Each part needs the other in order to function well. For instance, the head cannot function without the neck; neither can the hands function without the fingers and so on. Every part has a role to play for the common good of the whole body. In the same way, each one of us is important in the body of Christ, and each person can be used in different ways. Each one of us has something special to contribute that will edify God's people. Moreover, everyone has something that he or she can learn from others.

God made this lesson very clear to us on the day he paid a visit to Mnjala at their home. It was on a Sunday morning, and that day, they had no plans of going to church. Mnjala's mum had decided to take the day off and rest at home. She was planning to take it easy throughout the day.

While Mnjala was lying around in his bed, Jesus appeared to him. He said, "Mnjala, wake up and go to church. Do not just eat and sleep. And when you get to church, make sure you go to Sunday school so you can learn about Me."

Then Jesus left. Mnjala quickly ran to his mother's room to pass on this important message from our Lord. My sister Janet was so surprised. She called me and let me know that they were on their way to my house. She quickly got up and got herself and Mnjala ready to go to the house of the Lord. I need not say more. The instructions had come directly from the Lord. If you are in the habit of staying at home or occupying your time with other activities on Sundays, please change that habit and be obedient to the Lord. That day belongs to the Lord and should be set apart for Him.

> Remember the Sabbath day by keeping it holy. Six days you shall labor and do all your work, but the seventh day is a Sabbath to the Lord your God. On it you shall not do any work, neither you, nor your son or daughter, nor your manservant or maidservant, nor your animals, nor the alien within your gates. For in six days the Lord made the heavens and the earth, the sea, and all that is in them, but he rested on the seventh day. Therefore the Lord blessed the Sabbath day and made it holy (Exod. 20: 8–11).

Conversation with Angels

On this particular day, we were going to visit my parents-in-law. They were having a small party at their home to celebrate the success of their fiftieth anniversary celebration. Indeed, it is a good thing to look for great opportunities to celebrate. Mnjala was with us, so we all hopped into my car, and off we went, anticipating a wonderful afternoon. As I drove along, the children informed me that Angel Michael and Angel Gabriel were in the car with us. I asked, "Do you know how such big angels could fit in a small car like mine?"

Mungai responded, "The angels have said that God allows them to change sizes so as to fit into different places."

I directed my next question to the angels themselves.

"When were you angels created?"

Mungai answered, "The angels are telling us that God created them before the world was created."

We have already read that the angels existed at creation.

I asked, "Why is Satan so ugly yet he was created beautiful and lived in heaven?"

The children almost answered at the same time. "The angels have said that Satan wants to look ugly because he does not like anything that God created, including his own beauty. He was beautiful when he lived in heaven."

As you read in previous chapters regarding angels and demons, the word of God tells us that Satan was a beautiful being who worshipped God in heaven.

I drove silently to my parents-in-laws' home, thinking about the conversation I just had with the angels through the children. Everything they had said was true. The angels were in the car with us, and they were giving them the answers to my questions. I could hear the children giggling in the backseat of the car, but my thoughts were on every word they had spoken. In a short while, Mungai announced that Jesus had come to join us in the car and He had told them that He would stay with us until we got to his grandparents' house.

Chapter 18

God's Commandments Are Being Broken

Over the December school holidays, Mnjala came to stay with us for about two weeks. The two weeks were charged with stories about God, heaven, and hell. My life was being transformed every single day as I listened to them relating their experiences.

On this particular day, they recounted to me how Jesus had come and picked them up from their bed and how they had flown heavenward with Him holding their hands. When they got to the throne room, they found themselves wearing different garments.

They said, "We were wearing white robes with gold around the waist."

Then Jesus started to tell them that His commandments were being broken. He told them that people on earth were not keeping His rules. He began to show them how the commandments were being broken. They were looking down from heaven, and they could see what was happening on earth.

> They saw a man and a woman
> worshipping an idol. They were
> kneeling in front of this idol and pleading
> with it to answer their prayers.

Jesus showed them a man murdering another man by stabbing him in the stomach.

"At first, he seemed to be friendly to him, and then suddenly he drew a knife and stabbed him. Before stabbing him, he asked him to say his last prayer," Mnjala narrated.

Then they saw children telling lies to their parents. The children had stolen some money from a cupboard and hidden it in their pockets. When their father asked them where the money was, they responded that they did not know, yet the money was right there in their pockets.

Next, they saw a man and a woman worshipping an idol. The two were kneeling before this idol and pleading with it to answer their prayers. The woman kept saying to the statue that it should bring rain so the crops could grow.

"But the statue just stared right back at her with its mouth open. Like this." Mnjala opened his mouth wide. "They even tried to feed the idol with some food, but it did not eat anything."

The next picture was that of a woman being dishonest at her place of work. She had gone to work, but she did not complete her full day's work. She worked very briefly and then got into her car and drove off.

The children said they saw two thieves stealing from a bank. The thieves had guns in their hands. They stole and then ran off in a taxi while the police tried to catch up with them.

They were also shown a father and a mother arguing in their home. The father had stolen a television set from their neighbor, and the wife asked him about it. He got very angry with her for asking this so he started to beat her. He had asked his children to bring a shoe, which he used to beat his wife.

Jesus showed them an aircraft crashing. As it began to crash, the passengers in that plane hurriedly removed idols from their bags. They were praying to their idols, asking them not to let the plane crash, but all in vain. The plane crashed and killed many people, but those who escaped were bleeding profusely.

In the final part of the clip, Jesus showed them some children who spoke the truth to their parents. They had stolen some money, and when their father asked them about it, they admitted that they had taken it. Their father forgave them and told them that the truth had set them free.

In an earlier chapter, we saw how God gave the Ten Commandments to the Israelites as a guide for their daily lives. On a previous visit to heaven, God had requested Mungai and Mnjala to read the same commandments. It seems like God was already preparing their hearts to acknowledge that He Himself had written these rules or commandments with an expectation for people to honor and obey them.

These commandments are therefore applicable to our lives even today. They are not outdated as some people believe. God expects us to follow them so we are not only able to fellowship with Him but to also live together in peace and unity. Jesus summarized the Ten Commandments in the New Testament by saying we should love God and fellow men. "He answered: 'Love the Lord your God with all your heart and with all your soul and with all your strength and with all your mind'; and, 'Love your neighbor as yourself'" (Luke 10:27).

For three consecutive nights, Jesus showed the children the same visions of people on earth breaking His commandments. Thereafter, in the months that followed, He continued to show them that His commandments were still being broken, but He told them that He wants to forgive His people. Please ask the Lord to forgive you if you have been breaking any of His commandments.

Christmas in Heaven

As we were nearing Christmas, my son began telling me interesting stories about heaven. He told me that heaven had been decorated for Christmas with every house adorned with the words "Happy Birthday, Jesus." Mungai wanted us to decorate our house that way, too. I marveled at this. It seemed to me that many of things we do here on earth are a replica of what is done in heaven. I actually believe that earth copies from heaven. Mungai also informed me that Christmas carols were sung in heaven, too. They were sung in the throne room where God is.

On the actual day, Jesus visited early in the morning just as He had promised Mungai. He spent the day with us again. Mungai said he saw Jesus in his grandparents' living room. He was seated on one of the brown chairs and listening in on our conversations.

That night, Jesus took Mungai and Mnjala to heaven where there was a great celebration in honor of the birth of Our Lord Jesus Christ. There was food and cake, angels were singing, and the host of heaven were dancing and praising God. They were praising God for what He did for us. He sent His Only Son to save mankind so we can have eternal life in heaven. That is a lot to celebrate!

My mind was taken back to the story of the birth of Jesus here on earth over two thousand years ago. While the shepherds were watching their flock by night, an angel of God appeared to them to tell them the good news of the birth of Christ Jesus the Lord. As soon as the angel finished conveying the good news, a multitude of the heavenly host appeared with the angel, praising God.

> Suddenly a great company of the heavenly host appeared with the angel, praising God and saying, "Glory to God in the highest, and on earth peace to men on whom His favor rest." When the angels had left them and gone into heaven, the shepherds said to one another, "Let's go to Bethlehem and see this thing that has happened, which the Lord has told us about" (Luke 2:13–15).

This is proof that there was celebration in heaven at the birth of Jesus. The angels returned to heaven to continue with the party.

An Angel in Hospital

I was constantly reminded that angels always accompanied us. Everywhere we went, an angel seemed to be in our company, and my son could see him. Each time we entered our car to go somewhere, an angel was occupying an empty seat. Many times when we went to bed, an angel was guarding. By now, I had accepted the truth that God was always sending His angels to watch over us.

On this particular Friday evening, Mungai began to feel unwell. Right after dinner, he started complaining of a stomachache. I tried to get him to lie down, but he cried out in pain. I was not sure what to do. I knew I had to do something because his cry became more distressful. So I got him some medicine and a glass of water. In a very short while, he threw up. When he vomited the first time, he told me he felt better. So I put him to bed to sleep. In less than an hour, he had woken up and was throwing up again. This time, he became restless, and the vomiting continued.

He seemed to be in so much anguish that I decided to take him to a nearby hospital. It was now almost 10:00 p.m. I usually avoid driving at night, but I had no choice this day. I was alone with Mungai as my husband was away. As we approached the petrol station, I had this certainty that an angel was with us in the car. I felt silly asking, but I did.

Almost factually, I said," There must be an angel with us?" By this time, I had learned that they were always there.

Mungai responded in a weak voice, "Yes, Mum. Angel Gabriel is here." He pointed to the empty passenger's seat next to me. Mungai was seated in the back with our nanny. "He will make sure we get to the hospital. Do not worry."

It was so comforting to hear my son telling me this. The vomiting had become even worse, and I knew my little boy needed help. When we turned onto one of the streets, Mungai commented that Angel Gabriel was at the rear of the car pushing it so we could go faster. I must admit that I was driving a little faster than my usual speed.

When we got to hospital, the doctor examined him and wrote him a prescription. Mungai asked me whether he would be given an injection. I quickly brushed him off, not wanting to answer his question truthfully because I knew how much he feared the needle. As soon as we tried to leave the hospital, Mungai started throwing up again. The doctor and I decided that he should be given an injection to stop the vomiting. We remained in the hospital for another forty-five minutes for this to be done and for Mungai to get some rest.

On our way back home, Mungai said, "Mum, you did not tell me the truth about the injection. You know, Angel Gabriel had already told me that I was going to be given an injection. He stayed with me at the hospital, and he came back home with us."

Yes, God's angels watch over us! "The angel of the Lord encamps around those who fear Him, and He delivers them" (Ps. 34:7).

Jesus at a Hymn Concert

On December 5, 2010, Mungai and I went to the Nairobi Pentecostal Church in Nairobi for a hymn concert. My friend Zenah had invited us, as she was part of a singing group called the Glory Voices. This main group is comprised of thirteen female singers who are committed to leading people in worship during church services. They also minister God's Word to high school students. Each year, the Glory Voices recruit additional women, who they train to sing with them. This specific year, about seventy women formed the choir in this incredible hymn festival.

The concert began at about 3:00 p.m. Mungai and I sat in the balcony area of the church, and we were feeling the excitement that was in the air as people streamed into the sanctuary. We began by a word of prayer, followed by some praise and worship. Shortly after, the Glory Voices choir took the center stage, unleashing their angelic voices. I was enjoying every moment of it because I felt the hymns carry such powerful words of God's love and His salvation toward mankind. I was amazed by the fact that some of these hymns were written many centuries ago, and we still sing them to date. They never grow old or lose their power.

I sensed that Our Lord Jesus was in our midst because His Word says He dwells in the praises of His people.

Sure enough, Mungai confirmed this. "Mum, Jesus is here, and He has come with very many angels. He is standing in the center of the stage, right there where Aunty Zenah is standing." He pointed the location where our Lord was standing. "The angels are everywhere. Even outside the church, it is full of angels."

I was so excited! Once again, I was in awe of what the Lord was teaching me. I could not get over the fact that angels surrounded us and better still that Jesus was amongst us. How nice to be in the presence of the Lord! There could not have been a better place for me to have spent that afternoon other than in the midst of my Savior and Lord. I couldn't wait to tell Zenah that Jesus had come to the concert. Indeed, He had to show up because He has promised to be in the midst of every gathering that is done in His name.

Chapter 19

Jesus at an Overnight Prayer Meeting

On New Year's Eve 2010, my friend Zenah and I went for a watch-night service at the Nairobi Pentecostal Church in Nairobi. We wanted to usher in the New Year at church, praying and thanking God for His goodness. While we were at the service, the pastor announced that, if anyone wanted to give a testimony, he or she needed to write his or her name on a piece of paper and hand it over to a nearby usher. I felt in my heart to share something about what our Lord had shown the two cousins. I needed some kind of assurance that the feeling I had was divine. So I prayed in my heart and told God that, if He brought an usher near me, I would go ahead to speak to the congregation. The church was packed to capacity that night. There wasn't enough room to even move around. There had not been any usher near us for a long while, but suddenly like out of nowhere, this usher appeared behind me. I had to keep my promise to God, so I called the usher and submitted my name.

My heart was pounding. This was going to be the first time I would stand up and speak before such a big crowd of people. This particular church has a sitting capacity of approximately thirty-five hundred people, and it was completely packed that night with some people standing and others sitting on the stairway.

> Then Mungai told me, "I saw you in front of the church talking to the people about heaven and hell. Jesus was standing behind you, and He was whispering to you what to say."

My friend and I were seated upstairs, so we decided to move downstairs to be closer to the pulpit. This is where I was to stand to give my testimony. We had hardly sat down than my name was called out amongst the first five people to give their testimony. I went up to the podium and sat down. A lady, followed by two other people, gave their testimonies, and finally, it was my turn. I opted to move further down the queue and requested the pastor who was coordinating the session to allow me to wait for the other pastors to return from their tea break. I felt in my heart that I needed to speak while the pastors were in the service because it would encourage their hearts. A few of the pastors walked back in, so when it was my turn again, I stood up to speak. We had each been given only two minutes to speak, but I kindly requested for an additional five minutes. It is impossible to talk about these stories in five minutes. I wondered about which ones I was going to talk about and which ones I was going to leave out. I felt a little nervous at the beginning, but after a little while, a surge of confidence came over me, and I somehow knew what to say. The words kept coming into my heart, and I uttered them as quickly as I could.

I was so glad I had shared. Unspeakable joy suddenly filled my heart. I returned to my seat downstairs next to my friend, and some people around us requested that I tell them more of the stories. They had been encouraged by this word that was coming from the Lord. I was just a vessel that God had used to pass over His message.

What surprised me was what Mungai told me the following day. He had spent New Year's night at the home of my cousin Nzale, together with her husband Alex and their three daughters, Riziki, Zawadi, and Makena. I went to pick him up on New Year's Day sometime in the afternoon, but we only got to leave at about eight o'clock after having dinner with Nzale and her family.

As we were driving home, Mungai told me, "I saw you sharing in church about heaven and hell."

What is this boy talking about? I thought.

He explained to me that, when he went to sleep at Aunty Nzale's house, Jesus came to take him to heaven. Then he asked Jesus if he could see his mum first, and Jesus brought him to the church where we were. Isn't this amazing! Mungai went on to recount to me how Aunty Zenah and I were seated upstairs, and then we moved downstairs. He said he had seen some children with their parents, some of whom were tired and had fallen asleep. This was indeed an accurate description of the goings on at the watchnight service. Mungai did not make this up. The Lord showed it to him.

Then Mungai told me, "I saw you in front of the church talking to the people about heaven and hell. Jesus was standing behind you, and He was whispering to you what to say. Everything you said was what Jesus wanted the people to hear."

This was such a profound encounter not just for my son but for me. It confirmed to me that God had commissioned me to share His Word as He reveals it to these little children. I will endeavor to shout it from the mountaintop for everyone to hear and escape hell. The message is very clear. Heaven is real, and so is hell. There is no other way to escape hell except through Jesus Christ.

Annie's Mum Lives Heaven

On January 4, 2011, I received the dreaded message that informed us that Mrs. Phoebe Kigira, my sister-in-law's mum, had gone to be with the Lord. She had been ill for a long while and had been hospitalized for over two months. She had suffered from an infection after a surgery to correct her kidneys, but at the same time, her cancer had recurred. She was sixty-seven years old at the time of her passing away. We had all prayed and hoped for her healing, but it was now time for us to face the reality that God wanted her healed in heaven and not on earth.

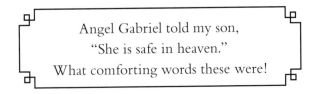

Angel Gabriel told my son,
"She is safe in heaven."
What comforting words these were!

During the funeral gathering, I got to understand that there are three types of healing. The first one is when God instantly touches you, and the healing occurs instantly. The second healing is when God tells you to wait, and He heals you at a later date. In such cases, it could take days, weeks, or even years before the healing occurs. During which time, God will teach you how to wait on Him. The third type of healing occurs in heaven after one has died. This means that one has to leave this body that is ailing and take up a new one that all those who believe in God take up once they die. Death for those who know the true God is just but moving from this residence to reside in heaven where God is.

As soon as we got the message of her passing on, Mungai's dad quickly rushed to the hospital to join Annie and other family members who had gathered there. Mungai and I joined them later. While on our way to hospital, Mungai told me that Angel Gabriel was in the car with us. I quickly asked him to ask the angel about Annie's mum.

Angel Gabriel told my son, "She is safe in heaven."

What comforting words these were!

> God allowed Mungai to see Annie's mum again on the third night in a row after her death. She was wearing a beautiful shining robe and singing and dancing to God in the throne room in heaven.

As soon as we arrived at the hospital, I hugged Annie and told her what Angel Gabriel had told Mungai. These words also comforted her. Her mother had made it to heaven, and that is the most important thing to happen to anybody. For those who believe in Jesus Christ, death of this body means being in the presence of God forever more.

We left the hospital and proceeded to Annie's home. Annie's children, Ryan and Trudy, took the news of their grandmother passing away very well. Ryan said his grandmother was lucky that she had gone to live in heaven. This was amazing to hear because those were Mungai's exact words when he initially heard the news. The children went off to play as we were left to make the funeral arrangements.

As we were leaving, Annie told Mungai to greet her mother for her when he goes to heaven. What is interesting is that this is exactly what happened.

That night, Mungai went to heaven, and he saw Phoebe in the throne room. He told me that she was shining so much and singing to God. He went over to her and told her, "Annie said hi to you."

She told Mungai, "Tell Annie I said hi back to her."

How my heart leapt with joy when I heard my son say these words to me. I quickly called my sister-in-law and shared the good news with her. We rejoiced in God despite our mourning. God brought such comfort to our hearts. I was happy about the fact that I had a chance to share the stories about heaven with Annie's mum. On one of my visits to hospital, we had talked about heaven. All we talked about that day was just heaven. Now she is living there, and my son saw her in her new home. What an honor and privilege.

The following night, Jesus took Mungai to heaven again, and he saw Annie's mum in the throne room again. This time round, she was dancing. She is obviously well in heaven. There is neither sickness nor disease in heaven.

God allowed Mungai to see Annie's mum again on the third night in a row after her death. She was wearing a beautiful shining robe and singing and dancing to God in the throne room. She is obviously very happy in heaven. There is no more pain or sorrow in heaven. On this night, God showed Mungai Annie's mother's house in heaven.

Mungai reported to me that her house is near the throne room. "Mum, I asked God to save me a house near the throne room, too."

I smiled.

In the beginning of the month of March 2011, Jesus picked Mungai from his bed and took him to heaven. This time, he was taken to Phoebe's house. He recounted how he entered her living room, which he described as being so beautiful. He said it has pictures around it, pictures of Annie, Trudy, Ryan, and Mungai.

"Mum, I did not visit the other rooms so I do not know whether there are more photos there. I found her seated on a beautiful shining sofa reading a book."

He told her, "Hi, Cucu."

She responded, "Hi, Mungai."

Then Jesus greeted her, too. Mungai said he stayed with her a little bit watching a big television set that she had in her house. He added that her house had a very big garden and a play park.

Mnjala told me that he had also seen Annie's mother in heaven many times. Once, he saw her in the throne room, and God the Father was telling her something. He could not hear what God was telling her. Then she went into the library in heaven to read.

Mnjala asked me, "Did she love reading books here on earth?"

"Yes, she did. She even wrote some books."

"She looked like she is twenty something, and she was wearing a very shiny robe."

Again, Jesus is teaching us something through this story. I hope you understand it. Life does not end here on earth. "He will wipe every tear from their eyes. There will be no more death or mourning or crying or pain for the old order of things has passed away" (Rev. 21:4).

Annie's Mum's Life Story

Annie's mother's full name is Phoebe Gloria Nyawira Kigira. She now lives in heaven. We miss her so dearly, but we are glad that we will see her again. It is not all over for her or for us. She is now living a glorious life in the presence of God forever.

After her passing on, we began to discover what kind of person she was, and we were astonished. She lived a very humble life, but she accomplished a lot for God's kingdom. She resigned from her job many years ago so she could serve God fully. During her ministry to God, she never gained any title, but God Himself ordained her as His minister. She was a wealthy woman according to the standards of the world, but you would have never known. She mingled with people from all walks of life. Whether you were rich or poor or young or old, she availed herself for you. She raised many men and women into places where they could administer the work of God. Many bishops, pastors, elders, and evangelists came to testify about her. They said she planted a seed in their hearts and taught them about discipleship. She was diligent and hardworking, and she loved the Lord with all her heart. She was dedicated to serving God, and she led many to the knowledge of Christ Jesus. She has left a legacy. She was a gallant soldier for our Lord Jesus, and she is now rejoicing in heaven with her God. Our dear mum Phoebe made it to heaven, and so shall you if you obey and live for the Lord Jesus.

We later learned that she had just finished writing a book before her passing away, *The Lordship of Jesus Christ: The Mark of a True Disciple.*

Our Lord Jesus had made a promise on Christmas day concerning Annie's mum saying that Annie would one day go home and find her healed. However, Annie's mum passed on. So, what did the promise really mean? My sister-in-law and I concluded that Jesus meant that she will, someday, see her mother in heaven healed. Heaven is the home that Jesus was referring to. Annie is looking forward to seeing her mum again. This is the hope that everyone who is in Christ Jesus has. We confirmed that this world is not our permanent home, we are just passing through.

Trudy's Story

On the last weekend of January, my nephew Ryan and niece Trudy came over to our house for a sleepover. On hearing that his cousins were coming to visit, Mungai said, "Mum, I asked Jesus whether I could go to heaven with my cousin Ryan and Jesus said yes."

Mungai reminded me, "When Jesus says yes, it is final. He does not change His mind."

Their mum dropped off the children as planned. As usual, they were very excited to be together to play, watch cartoons, and generally just exhaust themselves silly. No sooner had they arrived than they went off running to find activities to occupy themselves. Later that evening, we had dinner and said a prayer, and off we went to bed.

The following morning was one full of surprises. To begin with Mungai said excitedly, "Jesus visited at night and he took Ryan and me to heaven!"

"We passed through the planets with Ryan." Mungai added, almost breathless with excitement.

I looked at Ryan for some kind of explanation. "I cannot remember anything. Auntie Lyee, I slept so well. I have never slept so well like I did last night. I also woke up at the same time with Mungai."

Now that did it for me! My heart was pounding with excitement. I had had the same experience that very first time that I could not remember visiting heaven, yet Mungai had reported we had been together. That morning, we had woken up at the same time, and I had a very refreshed sleep. It was a very good and peaceful rest. I felt like I had slept like a baby. It was something I had never experienced before. My nephew Ryan was now telling me an exact version of my own story, only using different words. I immediately knew he had been to heaven with Mungai. Whether he remembered it or not, I was certain he had been to heaven.

Mungai told him that he saw his grandmother Phoebe and his Uncle Ken, who exclaimed, "Ryan, even you are here in heaven!"

"His grandmother was excited to see her grandchild, too," Mungai explained.

After all the excitement, we left for Mungai's school. Mungai is a member of the computer club at his school, and they meet on Saturday mornings. His cousins wanted to go along with him. As we were driving to school, Mungai was updating Ryan about their trip to heaven. Trudy was seated in the front seat next to me. She started to tell me something very interesting about heaven. At first, I thought she was trying to compete with her brother and cousin who were busy in the backseat of the car giggling and talking about their heaven adventure. But then she said something that made me realize that Jesus had also visited her.

This visit must have taken place sometime after their grandmother passed away, I thought.

In her sweet smile, she said, "I saw Cucu in heaven. God and Jesus were there with us, and they were shining so much that I had to try to cover my face. The light that comes from God and Jesus is so bright. And I was so happy to see my grandmother so I started to cry. My grandmother was also shining but not like Jesus."

"Did Jesus say anything to you?" I asked.

"Yes, He said He will visit me again another time."

"What about your grandmother. Did she say anything to you?"

"No, she did not. She was just looking at me and smiling."

"When did this happen?"

"As soon as my grandmother passed away."

By this time, Ryan was already filling me in on the story because his sister had already told him about it. He said, "On that day, Trudy woke up crying and our mum came into our room to find out what was happening but she did not quite understand the full story. She thought that something spooky had happened because all Trudy could say was, 'I have seen Cucu.'"[10]

The following day, when Trudy's parents came to my house to pick up the children, I let them know what Trudy told me. We analyzed the story and concluded that our Lord had visited Trudy. We were not sure whether she was taken to heaven or it was a vision that she saw, but we were certain she had a supernatural encounter. We were thankful to God, all the while certain that He wants to accomplish something special with children.

This, for me, was another confirmation that our souls live forever. We had already buried Cucu's body, but her spirit was alive in heaven with God. God had allowed Mungai to see her the same day she had passed away. God is teaching us through little children that those who die in Christ Jesus live forever in heaven.

Something to Ponder About

As you may have already figured out, this story is not about the two boys or their cousins. Neither is it about me, my sister, nor the fathers of these children. It is a story about God the Father and Jesus Christ, His Son. God in His greatness has chosen to reveal Himself through small children. He wants us to know that He is alive and well and He rules from on high. He has revealed Himself as the creator of the heavens and the earth and of everything in it, including you and me. God wants to have a relationship with you. He wants to be your Father. That is why

---

10 Cucu is the word for "grandmother" in the Kikuyu language, a dialect the Gikuyu people of Kenya speak.

he sent His only Son Jesus to die for you. It doesn't matter what you have done, where you live, your background, or your past or present life. God loves you so dearly. "Yet all who received him, to those who believed in His name, he gave the right to become children of God" (John 1:12).

For all who have become His children, God has prepared a place called heaven where we will go after death and live forever with Him. Mungai and Mnjala have seen this place several times. These boys do not live in the same home or same neighborhood, but Jesus picks them from their homes and takes them to heaven. In the morning, they both tell their mothers the same story. How awesome is this? The boys have described their experiences by saying that, when Jesus picks them up from their beds, they see their bodies still lying in the beds while their spirits go up to heaven together. Whichever way we look at it, we would have to admit that it is a supernatural encounter! Only the creator of this world can do something like this. His name is Jesus, and the Bible is His Word. Believe in Him today! You have nothing to lose but everything to gain.

The children have both said that, when they are in heaven, they do not want to return home because everyone in heaven is so happy and it is so much fun there. Once I was very sad to hear my son saying that he does not want to return home when he is in heaven. I asked him who would be my son if he did not return to me.

What about the people they have seen in heaven: Mary and Joseph, John the Baptist, the disciples of Jesus, Samuel, David, Moses, Abraham, and Sarah? These people lived on earth ages ago, but they are now in heaven. If you believe in the one true God and invite His Son Jesus into your heart, you, too, shall live in this wonderful place called heaven.

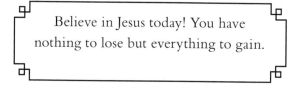

Believe in Jesus today! You have nothing to lose but everything to gain.

The children, as you have read, have also seen hell. They have seen Goliath of old, Michael Jackson, and many other people burning, crying, and suffering in the torments of hell. Hell is a place reserved for those who are not on the Lord's side, who continue to live in sin and in rebellion toward God's Word. "But the cowardly, the unbelieving, the vile, the murderers, the sexually immoral, those who practice magic arts, the idolaters and all liars—their place will be in the fiery lake of burning sulfur. This is the second death" (Rev. 21:8).

But God has given us hope, and this hope is in His Son, Jesus Christ.

The Way to the Father

God is our Father. There is only one way to Him, and it is through Jesus Christ Our Lord.

When we accept Jesus as the Son of God, we become God's children, and He becomes our father. We become co-heirs with Christ Jesus. What an honor! We have everlasting life in Him. This means that, when we die, we get to go to heaven and live with our Father forever and ever.

God is our Father, and Jesus is the only way to the Father.

Dear reader, there is no other way. There is no other truth. Jesus is the way to God. What has amazed me over the past two years is the fact that God has used my little son and nephew to prove Himself. It is incredible what we have learned from these two very young children. It has been made very clear in my mind who I am and who I belong to. I pray to God that this story will do the same to you. You belong to God. God made you. He made you for Himself, and He wants you to live for Him.

> Thomas said to Him, "Lord, we don't know where you are going, so how can we know the way?" Jesus answered, "I am the way and the truth and the life. No one comes to the Father except through me. If you really knew me, you would know my Father as well. From now on, you do know Him and have seen Him" (John 14:5-6).

Another Boy Called Colton

On May 6, 2011, my friend Angie sent me a text message in the middle of the night telling me she had bought a book online that she could not put down. She explained that the book was about heaven. Contained in the book was a story of a three-and-a-half-year-old American boy who had similar experiences to Mungai and Mnjala.

In the morning, eager to hear what she had to say, I called her.

She told me, "I went to sleep at three o'clock last night because I had to finish reading this book. It is called *Heaven Is for Real*. It is about a three-and-a-half-year-old American boy who Jesus showed heaven while he was in surgery. What is amazing is that your son's stories about heaven are very similar to this boy's!"

My heart was beating with excitement once again. God is awesome. He has used boys from different continents to express His love and His realness to us. I am also certain there are many more children He is and will be using to do the same. I made a point to read this book, and I was once again in awe.

This young boy called Colton Burpo had a near death experience just like my brother, Pastor Chola. Again, it proves to us that we are not just made out of body, but we have a spirit and soul. Our Lord Jesus held Colton on His lap while the doctors worked on his body that lay on the operating table. Angels were there, too, and they sang to the little boy. This reminded me of the time when my son Mungai was at the hospital and Angel Gabriel was there watching over him.

What Colton saw in heaven is indeed so similar to what my son and nephew have seen. Colton talked of angels with swords and the throne room of God. He even saw his great-grandfather who had passed away in 1976. Colton had never met his great-grandfather so he could only point him out from a photograph. However, even though his great-grandfather had died old and wrinkled, Colton could only recognize his face from the photo taken of him when he was very young because this was how he had seen him in heaven. He could not recognize his great-grandfather from the pictures taken when he was old and wrinkled.

Colton also saw a little girl whom he identified as his sister. His parents had never told the boy that his mother had a miscarriage when the pregnancy was only two months old. The parents did not even know that the child they had lost was a little girl until Colton told them that he saw her in heaven. Colton described the sister in heaven as resembling his older sister Cassie Burpo except she had black hair like their mum while Cassie had the same hair color as their dad. This little girl seemed to have grown in heaven. She was old enough to hug Colton. She told her brother that she could not wait for their dad and mum to get to heaven. A daughter they had never met was eagerly waiting for them in eternity.[11]

---

11 Burpo, *Heaven is for Real*, 2010.

How incredible! These boys, Colton, Mungai, and Mnjala, have never met, yet they have the same stories about heaven. Mungai and Mnjala live in Kenya in the continent of Africa while Colton lives in the United States of America! Please choose today to believe in and to live for this true God who lives in heaven. His Son Jesus is the way to heaven. There is no need to doubt. Just accept the truth. The truth is glaring in your face. Jesus loves you very much. He does not want you to end up in hell. But you have to choose Him. You have to put your trust and hope in Him.

Chapter 20

Jesus Is Light

On the night January 10, 2011, while deep asleep, I became aware of a very powerful presence that had surrounded me. This presence was full of love and felt like a warm embrace. Then I saw this brilliant light that was shining on me and on my son, who was in my bed with me.

The light shone so brightly that I whispered to myself, "Jesus, You are here."

The following day, Mungai pointed at where Jesus had stood that night in my room. It was exactly where the brilliant light was coming from.

Mungai said, "Mum, Jesus was standing here at night. He was shining so brightly, but He was careful not to blind us with His light."

I chuckled with mirth.

On January 22, 2011, we had a get-together at a friend's place in Ngong, an area in the outskirts of the city of Nairobi. We had formed a group of seven women called the Virtuous Women for the purpose of meeting together for prayer and fellowship. This time round, we decided to have a party at Anne's home. The day went very well with plenty of food, fun, and games. We also had a time of prayer together. I took this opportunity to share about Jesus and the visits from the Mighty King Jesus.

When the party was over, we got into our cars and commenced the somewhat long journey back to Nairobi. Esther and I were in the same car together with her son Shawn and my son Mungai. As we drove, Esther and I were having small talk while Shawn and Mungai were also having their share of talking in the back of the car. Their conversation was definitely more interesting than ours was.

Shawn was inquiring from Mungai about Jesus and heaven. He had plenty of questions. "Do you still go to heaven? Does heaven shine? How does Jesus look?" Then he said longingly, "I wish I could see Jesus."

Mungai gave him short answers like, "Yes, Jesus shines. Yes, heaven is beautiful."

Then we heard our two sons making comments about the sky and noting how it was full of stars.

After a short while, Mungai told Shawn, "Can you see that light between those two stars?"

"Yes."

"Can you see the light is following us?"

"Yes."

"That is Jesus."

Shortly, Mungai exclaimed with excitement, "Jesus is here! Jesus is here!"

Esther asked me, "What do we do? Jesus is here with us?"

I had no words for her. In truth, an overwhelming feeling engulfs one when you hear that Jesus is around. You believe it, yet you cannot see Him. So we just drove in silence, amazed at what was taking place. We praised God that He had visited us. I said a thanksgiving prayer in my heart.

When we got home, I asked Mungai, "How did you know that the light between the two stars was Jesus?"

"I knew the same way I always do." He pointed at his heart. "Here, I knew in my heart that it was Jesus."

He continued to explain, "The light became so big, and then it came down towards us from the sky and entered the car. The light then turned into Jesus. This is when I told you that Jesus was with us."

Jesus is light! I thought to myself.

Jesus is the light of the world. He came to bring light to us. His light brings life. He came to bring life to His creation. "Through Him all things were made; without Him nothing was made that has been made. In Him was life, and that life was the light of men. The light shines in the darkness, but the darkness has not understood it" (John 1:3–5). "For with you is the fountain of life, in your light we see light" (Ps. 36:9).

About Jesus

There is no question that Jesus exists. The Bible says He is seated at the right side of our Father in heaven. There has been a general agreement in many history books that Jesus lived in this world over two thousand years ago. Most religions say that Jesus was a prophet or a good teacher, but He definitely was not an ordinary man. He was more than a man. He is God. He healed the sick, cleansed the lepers, cast out demons, walked on water, turned water into wine, and preached about the kingdom of God. The Bible teaches us that Jesus was much more than just a prophet or teacher who performed many miracles.

Old Testament prophesies revealed the deity of Jesus. "For to us a child is born, to us a son is given, and the government will be on His shoulders. And He will be called Wonderful Counselor, Mighty God, Everlasting Father, and Prince of Peace" (Isa. 9:6). Jesus claimed to be God, and He is God. He and God are one. "I and the Father are one" (John 10:30).

The Jews wanted to stone Jesus for claiming that He was God, and Jesus did not deny the claim. In describing the deity of Jesus, the apostle John explained that Jesus was the Word right from the beginning together with God, and this Word became flesh and dwelt among us.

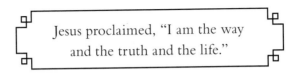

Jesus proclaimed, "I am the way and the truth and the life."

"In the beginning was the Word and the Word was with God and the Word was God. He was with God in the beginning" (John 1:1-2). Jesus is not God's son in the way we know it in the human sense. Jesus was conceived through the Holy Spirit and was carried in the womb of a woman called Mary. Jesus is God in human form.

The most important reason that Jesus has to be God is that, if He were not God, then His death would not have been sufficient to pay the penalty for the sins of the world. Had he been a created being and not God, then He could not have paid the infinite penalty required for sin against an infinite God. Only God can pay such an infinite penalty for sin because He alone is holy. Only God could take on all the sins of this world, die, and be resurrected, proving His victory over sin and death. "God made Him who knew no sin to be sin for us, so that in Him we might become the righteousness of God" (2 Cor. 5:21).

Jesus had to be God in order to pay for our sins. Jesus had to be man so He could die. Salvation is only available through faith in Jesus Christ. Jesus' deity is why He is the only way of salvation. Jesus' deity is why He proclaimed, "I am the way and the truth and the life. No one comes to the Father except through me" (John 14:6). What did Jesus mean by this?

- **The way.** Jesus stated that He is the only way. Jesus urged His followers many times that they should follow Him. There is no other path or route one can take to heaven. Jesus is the only way to the Father. Peter, the Lord's disciple, emphasized this truth in the book of Acts when He preached to the rulers in Jerusalem when talking about Jesus. "Salvation is found in no one else, for there is no other name under heaven given to men by which we must be saved" (Acts 4:12). The only path to salvation is expressed in the words "I am the way."

- **The truth.** Again, Jesus used the definite article "the" to emphasize that He alone is "the only truth." Psalm 119:142 says, "Your law is the truth." Jesus is the genuine God. He is the real Lord. There is no other true God. It is through Him that we will get eternal life.

- **The life.** Jesus claimed to be the source of all life. In John 10:17–18, He declared that He was going to die for us all and then rise again. Only God has authority over life and death. That is why Jesus died and rose again. To His followers, He promised "because I live, you also will live."

In the same way His disciples followed Him years ago, we, too, can follow Him today. The disciples believed that Jesus had died to take the punishment of their sins and rose from the dead to give them new life. In so doing, they confessed their sins and endeavored to put into practice what He had taught them about righteousness. They proclaimed the good news around the world telling others the truth about sin, righteousness, and judgment. This same Jesus is "the way" today. We have hope in Him.

No other religion offers the infinite payment of sin that only Jesus Christ can provide. No other "religious founder" was God became man and sacrificed His life in order to save all the people of the world. There is power in the blood that Jesus shed. This blood cleanses us from all sin. "He is the atoning sacrifice for our sins, and not only for ours but also for the sins of the whole world" (1 John 2:2).

A Word for the Backslider

A backslider is someone who had once accepted Jesus and then, turned his or her back on Him somewhere along the way. A backslider is one who has left the narrow road and started to walk on the wide road that leads to destruction. If you are one of those, please return to the Master. Do not allow Satan, the deceiver, to lead you to hell. It is not worth it. Whatever sin that caused you to fall back is not worth you going to hell for. The torments of hell are terrible. You cannot exchange the so-called earthly pleasures for an eternity of torment and punishment with Satan and his demons in hell. Do not let Satan have the last laugh! Jesus is waiting for you to come back to Him. His arms are wide open just for you. It does not matter what sin you have committed. Just genuinely ask Him to forgive you, and He will. He is the only one who can forgive you. He is the only one who has the key to heaven.

In Luke 15, three parables are told: the Parable of the Lost Sheep, the Parable of the Lost Son, and the Parable of the Lost Coin. These are told to show us how God cherishes even just one sinner who repents and returns to Him. There is ecstatic rejoicing in heaven!

> Now the tax collectors and sinners were all gathering around to hear Him. But the Pharisees and the teachers of the law muttered, "This man welcomes sinners and eats with them." Then Jesus told them this parable; "Suppose one of you has a hundred sheep and loses one of them. Does he not leave the ninety-nine in the open country and go after the lost sheep until he finds it? And when he finds it, he joyfully puts it on his shoulders and goes home. Then he calls his friends and neighbors together and says, 'Rejoice with me, I have found my lost sheep.' I tell you that in the same way there will be more rejoicing in heaven over one sinner who repents than over ninety-nine righteous persons who do not need to repent. Or suppose a woman has ten silver coins and loses one. Does she not light a lamp, sweep the house and search carefully until she finds it? And when she finds it, she calls her friends and neighbors together and says, 'Rejoice with me, I have found my lost coin. In the same way, I tell you there is rejoicing in the presence of the angels of God over one sinner who repents'" (Luke 15:1–9).

Backslider, God wants you back. Please come back to Him. Resist the devil, and he will flee from you. Resist all temptation to remain in sin. The consequences are grave. Make that choice right now while you still have the breath of life in you because, once you die, that will be the end of you. You will have to live in hell forever and ever. Nobody who is already in hell can escape. The time is now!

Whosoever

God loves you. Yes, you, whoever you are, whether big or small, rich or poor, tall or short. He loves you regardless of your race, your country of origin, whether you have much or little, or whether you eat with kings or just have an ordinary life. He loves you just the way you are. He created you. He knew you even before you were conceived in your mother's womb. His greatest desire is that you have a relationship with Him. God wants you to believe in Him and to live in obedience to His word.

- "For God so loved the world that He gave His only Son that whoever believes in Him shall not perish but have eternal life" (John 3:16).
- "For whoever finds me finds life and receives favor from the Lord. But whoever fails to find me harms himself; all who hate me love death" (Prov. 8:35–36).
- "Whoever believes in the Son has eternal life, but whoever rejects the Son will not see life, for God's wrath remains on him" (John 3:36).

God does not have any favorites; "whosoever" means any person. Jesus died for all of us, and He loves everyone in the same way. Ours is just to believe in His name, believing He redeemed us by His blood.

Prayer of Salvation

We have all committed sin against God. Nobody has lived a perfect life. "For all have sinned and fall short of the glory of God" (Rom. 3:23). All you need to do is believe. Believe that God sent Jesus to die for your sins. Believe you will have eternal life in Him, just as God has promised in the Bible. "That if you confess with your mouth, "Jesus is Lord," and believe in your heart that God raised Him from the dead, you will be saved" (Rom. 10:9).

Whereas man was created to be friends with God, he chose to go his own way, and the friendship with God was broken. Sin is when man rebels against God and is not concerned about Him. Sin is when he does not live up to God's perfect standards. For this reason, man is separated from God because God is holy, whereas man is sinful so there is a huge separation between the two. Man tries to reach God through his own efforts—living a good life, doing charity works, being religious, and so forth—but all his efforts fail. "For the wages of sin is death (spiritual separation from God) but the gift of God is eternal life in Christ Jesus our Lord" (Rom. 6:23).

Jesus Christ is the only way man can reach God. Only through Him can one know God and experience His love and plan for your life. "For Christ died for sins once for all, the righteous for the unrighteous, to bring you to God. He was put to death in the body but made alive by the Spirit" (1 Pet. 3:18).

God has bridged this separation between Himself and us by sending His own Son, Jesus Christ, to die on the cross in our place. "But God demonstrates His own love for us in this: While we were still sinners, Christ died for us" (Rom. 5:8).

It is not enough to have head knowledge of these facts or to agree with Christ's teachings. We must each receive Jesus Christ as Savior and Lord. We must believe and receive Christ by faith. All you need to do is believe. Believe that God sent Jesus to die for your sins. Believe that you will have eternal life in Him, just as God has promised in the Bible. "Yet to all who received Him, to those who believed in His name, He gave the right to become children of God" (John 1:12). "For it is by grace you have been saved through faith – and this is not from yourselves, it is the gift of God – not by works, so that no one can boast" (Eph. 2:8–9).

We receive Christ by inviting Him into our heart. Do make a decision by saying the prayer below and mean it from the bottom of your heart. The prayer below is just a guide. What is important is that you believe, repent, and confess Christ. "That if you confess with your mouth, "Jesus is Lord," and believe in your heart that God raised Him from the dead, you will be saved" (Rom. 10:9).

Dear Lord Jesus, I am a sinner. I have sinned against you. I ask that you forgive me and make me a new creature. Wash away all the sins of my past, and make me as white as snow. I believe you died on the cross so I can be made whole and set free from the penalty of sin and death. Thank you that you love me just as I am with an everlasting love. From today onwards, I want to live my life for you. I want to begin a new chapter of my life. I open the door of my heart and let you in. Take control of my life. Watch over all the affairs of my life. Thank you that now I am assured of eternal life in heaven so that where you are, I may be also. I ask you to fill me with Your Holy Spirit so He may walk with me and teach me your ways. In Jesus' name I pray. Amen.

If you have said this prayer and meant it in your heart, you are now God's child. You are now born again or saved, as the Bible puts it. It is that simple. The price was paid for you on the cross. Your sins have been forgiven, and you have now begun a new life with Christ as your Master. Your old self is gone, and now a new you has begun. Your past is gone. It is forgotten. Do not let anyone remind you of it. The Bible confirms this. "Therefore, if anyone is in Christ, he is a new creation, the old has gone, the new has come!" (2 Cor. 5: 17).

About the Holy Spirit

When we are born again, the Holy Spirit comes to live in us. The Holy Spirit is a person. He is part of the trinity that comprises of God the Father, God the Son, and God the Holy Spirit. When we receive the Holy Spirit, we are inviting God to be a part of us, and we allow ourselves to be a part of God. In 1 Corinthians 6:19, apostle Paul teaches: "Do you not know that your body is a temple of the Holy Spirit, who is in you, whom you have received from God?"

When Jesus was with His disciples, He explained to them that He would send them a helper upon His departure to heaven. This helper is the Holy Spirit, whose role is to guard, teach, comfort, and counsel His followers. This promise is not just for the disciples. It is for us, too. Jesus taught this of the Holy Spirit. "And I will ask the Father and He will give you another Counselor to be with you forever—the Spirit of truth. The world cannot accept Him, because it neither sees Him nor knows Him. But you know Him for He lives with you and will be in you" (John 14:16-17).

The Holy Spirit has come to live with you now that you have received Jesus Christ as your personal Savior. He is God and has several roles within the Trinity. The Holy Spirit makes us Christ-like. He helps us emanate characteristics that resemble the ones of Jesus Our Lord. People begin to see a change in our manners. The fruit of His spirit is love, kindness, gentleness, honesty, joy, peace, and righteousness. The Holy Spirit is a teacher. He teaches us things about God. He also brings into remembrance whatever God has taught us. He makes a quickening in our spirits that aligns our thoughts to His. "But the Counselor, the Holy Spirit, whom the Father will send in my name, will teach you all things and will remind you of everything I have said to you" (John 14:26).

The Holy Spirit directs us and shows us the ways of God. We are able to hear from God because of His spirit that is in us. In many instances, the prophets of old and those of today are able to predict what is to come because the Holy Spirit reveals this to them. For example, the birth of Jesus was predicted through Isaiah, the prophet of God. How could this prophet have predicted such a thing centuries before it came to pass? It was through the Spirit of God! "But when He, the Spirit of Truth, comes, He will guide you into all truth. He will not speak on His own; He will speak only what He hears and He will tell you what is yet to come" (John 16:13).

The Holy Spirit also helps us in prayer. The word of God says the Spirit helps us in our weakness when we do not know what to pray for. He intervenes by interceding for us in accordance with God's will. He works together with God the Father who searches our hearts. Because the Father knows the mind of the Spirit who is praying on our behalf, He goes ahead to answer our prayers (Rom. 8:28–29).

When Our Lord Jesus was about to ascend to heaven, he promised His disciples that He would send them a helper, a counselor who would be with them forever. On the day of Pentecost, the Holy Spirit fell on the disciples, who were in an upper room in Jerusalem. This incident is recorded in Acts 1. When the Holy Spirit came upon the disciples, they began to speak in different tongues as the Spirit enabled them. After this experience, they received power and were courageous to spread the gospel of Jesus Christ. This experience is described as the baptism of Holy Spirit.

> But the Counselor, the Holy Spirit,
> whom the Father will send in my name,
> will teach you all things and will remind you
> of everything I have said to you.

Once you repent your sins and receive Jesus in your heart, you have the right to ask for the baptism of the Holy Spirit. The baptism of the Holy Spirit is received by faith. Salvation is also received by faith in God. The word of God says that, whatever we ask according to His will, He hears us. Ask Jesus right now to fill you with His Holy Spirit and He will! Baptism in the Holy Spirit is usually a controversial subject in Christendom. I would like to share my personal experience in this regards. I had been in Christ for several years then one day at an evening church service in a Pentecostal church, a preacher asked that those who would like to be baptized by the Holy Spirit should go to the altar for prayers. I was afraid to go to the altar because sometimes people would fall flat on the floor during such prayers. I repeated the prayer that the preacher had asked us to say after him. Right where I stood, I started to speak in a different language. I had been baptized by the Holy Spirit. You too, can receive this baptism.

Jesus Will Come Back Soon

While He was on earth, Jesus promised He would come back again for His people. We have already learned that He keeps His word.

Behold I am coming soon! My reward is with me, and I will give to everyone according to what he has done. I am the Alpha and the Omega, the First and the Last, the Beginning and the End. Blessed are those who wash their robes, that they may have the right to the tree of life and may go through the gates into the city.

Outside are the dogs, those who practice magic arts, the sexually immoral, the murderers, the idolaters and everyone who loves the practices falsehood. I, Jesus, have sent my angel to give you this testimony for the churches. I am the Root and the Offspring of David, and the bright Morning Star (Rev. 22:12–16).

Only God the Father knows the date and time of Jesus' return. The Bible says Jesus will come back at the "twinkling of an eye," which means in a split second. He will be back to snatch all those who belong to Him. He will obviously recognize them because it will be those who will have believed in Him, repented of their sins, and are walking according to His commandments. He will take those ones away to heaven.

Friends, be prepared for the coming of the Lord. Remember that you need to be ready always. Do not live in sin and expect to be taken to heaven. Jesus showed the children that His commandments are being broken. Who is breaking them? If you are one of those people living in sin and yet claim you are a follower of Jesus, please beware. God sees our every move, our thoughts, our hearts, our deeds, and our intentions. God cannot be deceived; neither can He be mocked. You can lie to those who are living around you, but you cannot lie to God. He can see you. Do not let Satan have his way in your life. If you have been living in sin, ask Jesus to forgive you, and He will. He wants to forgive you. He will forgive and forget all your sins. "If we confess our sins he is faithful and just and will forgive us our sins and purify us from all unrighteousness" (1 John 1:9).

When the trumpet sounds on the day of the Lord's return, there will be no time to run; neither will there be time to repent. You will either be found ready or not. Please get ready now!

No one knows about that day or hour, not even the angels in heaven, or the Son but only the Father. Be on guard! Be alert! You do not know when that time will come. It's like a man going away: He leaves his house and puts his servants in charge, each with his assigned task, and tells the one at the door to keep watch. Therefore keep watch because you do not know when the owner of the house will come back—whether in the evening or at midnight, or when the rooster crows, or at dawn. If he comes suddenly, do not let Him find you sleeping. What I say to you, I say to everyone: "Watch!" (Mark 13:32–37).

A Concluding Remark

The people who are in heaven have something in common. They all believed in the one true God and Jesus Christ, His only son. Uncle Ken, Annie's mother, Pastor George's grandmother, and the New Testament Christians all believed in Jesus. The blood that Jesus shed on the cross at Calvary washed away their sins. The Old Testament folk believed in the one true God and did not worship idols. This true God later sent His Son Jesus on earth to come and die for us that He may reconcile all men to Himself.

Pastor George's grandmother died in February 2010, and Mungai saw her in heaven with Jesus. Mungai had never met her, but he told me, "Mum, when I saw Pastor George's grandmother in heaven, I knew it was her. Jesus was holding her hand. Nobody had to tell me who she was. I knew it in my heart."

In the same manner, the people in hell are there because they have something in common. The following passage in the Bible sums it up perfectly: "Whoever believes in the Son has eternal life; but whoever rejects the Son will not see life, for God's wrath remains on them" (John 3:36).

During the festive season of December 2010, the boys, together with me, and my friend Zenah went to share the heaven encounters with one of her colleagues and her parents visiting from Scotland. I narrated to them a few stories from the children's visits to heaven and hell, but her father did not believe them to be true. According to him, there is no life after death, that life ends right here on earth upon one's death. Later on after we had left, Mnjala told us that Jesus had been right there in the center of the living room when I was sharing their stories, but He nodded sadly when the white man refused to believe in Him.

On another occasion, while taking a walk with Mungai, he surprised me by suddenly asking me to go and tell a friend of his about Jesus. I did not know which friend he was referring to, but he immediately told me that it was the guard who worked in one of the houses in the neighborhood.

He insisted, "Mum, you need to tell him about Jesus so he can make it to heaven. You know he is an old man and could die anytime. If he died, I would like to find him in heaven!"

What my son was asking me to do so surprised me. He kept insisting that we had to tell everyone we know about Jesus. This surprised me because he was a young child, but despite his age, he was deeply aware of the importance of telling people about Jesus because of the consequences of unbelief.

I was hesitant to talk to the old man. I had never talked to a Muslim about Jesus. My son saw my hesitation.

Concerned, he said, "Mum, Yusuf [not his real name] is my friend. He is very nice and kind to me. He lets me ride my bike around his compound, and sometimes he helps me pump my flat tires. He also has a bike. You want my friend to go to hell? I have seen hell, and it is a very bad place. I do not want my friend to go to hell."

My little boy was almost in tears as he continued to insist that his friend needed to know the Lord. So I promised to talk to him.

The following day, I prepared a meal for Yusuf and went up to greet him. I had met him many times during our walks with Mungai around our neighborhood. He was very grateful for the tasty meal. I told him that Mungai had sent me to tell him about Jesus and proceeded to relate how Our Lord Jesus had visited him several times and showed him heaven and hell.

"Mungai has told me that he does not want you to go to hell. He wants you to know that the gate to heaven is Jesus," I said gently but with confidence.

I explained how Our Lord Jesus started visiting Mungai and Mnjala and the incredible experiences the two children had had. I also told him how much God loved him. Yusuf was amazed, but more importantly, he believed. He lifted both his hands up and declared that he believed. I then led him through repentance, and he accepted Christ.

He confessed to me that his wife and children were Christians, but he was the only Muslim due to his family background. I thank God that he is now God's child, having chosen Jesus!

Who will you choose to believe in today? The choice is yours. Do not wait for tomorrow, for nobody knows what tomorrow will bring. This could be your last day on planet Earth. After this, you will have to step into eternity. Where will you spend eternity? Will you spend it in heaven or in hell? Please make the right choice for yourself, because as you were born alone, you will also surely die alone. Do not make this choice based on what your family or friends think. They, too, need to decide their destinies. The world's philosophies and New Age religions will not save you. There is only one gate to heaven. It is through Jesus Christ, the one and only true God. Let nothing or anyone come between you and heaven. The price would be too costly!

The kingdom of heaven is like treasure hidden in a field. When a man found it, he hid it again, and then in his joy, he went and sold all he had and bought that field. Again, the kingdom of heaven is like a merchant looking for fine pearls. When he found one of great value, he went away and sold everything he had and bought it.

(Matthew13:44)

About the Author

My name is Lydia Nzale Chola-Waiyaki. I was born and raised in Nairobi, Kenya. I am the fourth born in a family of seven children (one brother and five sisters). We grew up in a Christian home. Both my parents took us to Sunday school, and when we were older, they took us to church every Sunday. My mother is very prayerful. She always prayed for my siblings and me. She also taught us about Jesus when we were growing up. She bought us children's Bible books and read the word of God to us. I always enjoyed Sunday school, and when I was older, I would accompany my parents to church. I loved Jesus, and I knew from a very young age that He is God.

When I was in high school, I continued to attend church every Sunday. I knew in my heart that I believed totally in Christ, but I made a fresh commitment to salvation when I went to university. My relationship with Jesus grew when I was at my university because I met many young people who loved the Lord. One person I met at the time who influenced my life positively is my friend, Zenah Nyathama. She helped me grow in the Lord. I continued to serve the Lord throughout my young adult life. My husband, who I also met at my university, also loved the Lord. We were married a few years later.

After graduating from university, I got a job with an international nongovernmental organization that assists refugees in Africa. I have enjoyed working with this organization because my job there was a prayer that God answered to the letter. I like working with vulnerable groups because I find fulfillment in helping people in need.

After a year of marriage, our son, Mungai, was born in 2002. It was a joy to welcome him into the world. I never could have imagined that God would use this son of mine to bring me even closer to Himself. Moreover, never could I have ever dreamed that God would choose my son to tell the world that heaven and hell are real places.

Despite my family being committed Christians and taking us to church, I was your regular young person. I enjoyed hanging out with my friends. I wanted to fit in and generally led a pretty normal life. I was never engaged enough in anything spiritual to warrant me being branded a zealous Christian. As an adult, I have been your regular wife and mother, going about life in the best way I know how. It therefore came as a complete surprise to me when I realized that God had set me up to spread His Word to the outermost parts of the world by bringing the supernatural right into my home.

Since our Lord Jesus started visiting my son, I have grown in the Lord in leaps and bounds. I have immersed myself in reading the Bible and various spiritual materials so as to be able to understand and confirm the authenticity of the visions. Everything about me has changed: my dreams, plans, perspective toward life, motives, attitudes, values, and relationships with family, friends, and society as a whole. I enjoy talking about Jesus because I want everyone to know Him. I want as many people as possible to make it to heaven!

I hope that this book has blessed you. If you prayed the prayer of salvation and meant it in your heart, you are now a Christian. Welcome to the family of God! "Yet to all who received Him, to those who believed in His name, He gave the right to become children of God—children born not of natural descent, nor of human decision or a husband's will, but born of God" (John 1:12–13).

References

Baxter, Mary K. *A Divine Revelation of Hell*. New Kensington: Whitaker House, 1993.

Burpo, Todd, with Lynn Vincent. *Heaven is for Real*. Nashville: Thomas Nelson Publishers, 2010.

En.wikipedia.org/wiki/Halloween

En.wikipedia.org/wiki/Near-death_experience

Gilgio, Louie. *Indescribable.2008[YouTube]* http://www.youtube.com/watch?v=ewKtSKbWZUI

Hunter, Charles, and Frances. *The Angel Book: Personal Encounters with God's Messengers*. Kingwood: Hunter Books, 1999.

Lewis, G. Craig. *The Truth About Hip Hop*. X-Ministries, 2008. [DVD]

Liardon, Roberts. *We Saw Heaven*. Tulsa: Insight Publishing Group, 2000.

Spiritlessons.com/Documents/7_Jovenes/English_7_Jovenes_ Revelations of Heaven and Hell to 7 Columbian Youths_Text.htm

Spiritlessons.com/Documents/Angelica Zombrano_Prepare to meet your God/Index_Text.htm

Spiritlessons.com/Documents/Bill Wiese_23 Minutes in Hell_ Text.htm

The Holy Bible, New International Version. Grand Rapids: Zondervan, 2005.

www.amightywind.com/hell/testimonies.htm

www.GotAnyQuestion? Bible questions answered.